I0031150

# The Profitable
# BOOKKEEPING BUSINESS
## Pricing, Growth and Workflow

Renee Minchin

**The Profitable Bookkeeping Business**
**Pricing, Growth and Workflow**

First published in Australia by Conscious Bias 2025
Books That Rewire
www.reneeminchin.com

A catalogue record for this
book is available from the
National Library of Australia

ISBN: 978-1-7641133-0-4 (pbk)
ISBN: 978-1-7641133-1-1 (ebk)

Front cover design: Marco Ohmer © (shutterstock)

Typesetting and design by Publicious Book Publishing
Published in collaboration with Publicious Book Publishing
www.publicious.com.au

# Table of Contents

# The Profitable Bookkeeping Business: Pricing, Growth, and Workflow

# Introduction

So, you've decided to start your own bookkeeping business. Congratulations on taking the first steps on the exciting and rewarding journey to starting your own successful business.

When you decide to start a new business, it seems like the list of things to do is never ending – from choosing a business name and getting set up legally, to opening a business bank account, registering for taxes, and creating an online presence to attract clients. And that's before you even get onto things like creating your branding, developing your product or service offering, and marketing yourself to potential customers!

Starting a new business can seem like a daunting and overwhelming prospect sometimes, especially if you've never done so before. And whilst it's true that setting up your own business can be a lot of hard work, it can be incredibly rewarding too.

My hope is that this guide will help to eliminate some of the guesswork by telling you a lot about what you need to know to be able to set up your own successful bookkeeping business.

## My journey

I'm Renee Minchin and I'm an Australian CFO, accountant, bookkeeper, BAS (business activity statements) agent, ASIC (Australian Securities and Investments Commission) agent, mentor, and business owner. Having been in the industry for over 20 years, I've certainly picked up plenty of tips and tricks along the way. In this book, I'll be telling you what I know and giving you all the know-how you need to make your dreams of starting a thriving bookkeeping business a reality.

I wanted to write this book to support other bookkeepers who have always dreamed of setting up their own practice. I know that when I was first starting out, I found myself feeling really overwhelmed and not knowing where to start. Ultimately, this led to me wasting a lot of time and money on things that I did not need and which had no benefit to my business. I know I would have found it helpful learning from someone who had walked the path before me; someone who had already discovered through trial and error what works and what doesn't. That insight is what I am hoping to offer you with this book.

# Section 1: Why Start a Business? Finding Your Why

# Chapter 1: Create Your Vision

Just as with any kind of business, the first step to building a successful bookkeeping business is to create your vision. A common misconception is that only larger companies and businesses have a vision. However, a clear and well-defined vision is a must-have for any business, no matter how big or small.

Having a clear vision in place will help you to stay on track to achieving your goals, even if you lose sight of them briefly along the way. As Steve Jobs said: *"You can't connect the dots looking forward; you can only connect them looking backwards."* And it's true – looking back on your business journey, you'll always be able to see the path, but that path might seem less clear when you look ahead to the future. Your vision is what helps you to connect these dots and find the right path to bring you closer to achieving your business goals.

If you haven't already decided on your vision, it's time to create one. In my opinion, this should always be the first thing you do whenever you set out on a new business venture so that you know your "why" – that is, your meaning or purpose, or why it is that you do what you do.

For the bookkeeping side of my business, my "why" was to create freedom. I wanted to set up a business where I was able to scale, without the business relying on me to complete everything personally. On the mentoring side, my "why" was to educate others, whilst still affording me that sense of freedom as well. I set it up so I could work the hours I wanted, whilst giving back to fellow bookkeepers by passing on some of the skills and knowledge I had learned over the years.

There are a few other things that you will need to keep in mind when crafting the perfect vision statement, such as your goals, your point of difference, and your values. All of these will shape the direction in which you take your bookkeeping business, and therefore will influence the kind of vision that you set for yourself.

**What are your goals?**

Your vision should basically be your goal for where you want your bookkeeping practice to get to. Take a big picture view of the next three to ten years, and think about what exactly it is you want your business to achieve during this time. For example:

- Do you want to offer a range of different services, or do you want to hone in on just a few?

- Do you want to scale and grow bigger in size, or do you want to be more of a boutique practice that works with a smaller group of clients?

- Is there a particular niche, industry, or type of client that you want to focus on?

- What is it that you want to help your clients achieve, or how are you going to help them improve their lives and their businesses? Do you want to help them save time, be less stressed, make more money, or achieve financial freedom?

- Do you want to become an influencer or thought leader in your industry?

For example, your goal might be to offer a comprehensive range of different bookkeeping, accounting, and business advisory services in your business so you can become your clients' one-stop-stop for everything to do with their finances. In this case, your vision would look vastly different to a bookkeeper whose goal for their business is to hone in on two or three services and position themselves as a specialist in these areas.

For me, my goal started off as freedom. Now, it's freedom and flexibility. Freedom for me meant being able to work the hours I want so I could start and raise a family. It also meant being able to earn an income which reflected my value, whilst building an asset and enjoying what I do.

A big one for me too was that I wanted to create a business that supports other families. To this day, my business has a big focus on family. We have a saying – family comes first – and that applies not only to me, but to all staff with flexible working arrangements. Whether it's children's sport days, taking animals to appointments, or even getting dinner in the oven, flexibility means being able to prioritise what matters in your life.

Whatever your goals and aspirations, your answers to these questions will help you to come up with the vision for your bookkeeping business.

## What's your point of difference?

Your vision should also reflect your point of difference, or what exactly it is that makes your bookkeeping practice stand out from the rest. This plays a big part in creating your overall brand, and will play a role in how you present yourself in every touchpoint that you have with your clients.

What is it that makes you unique? For example, are you an industry leader or subject matter expert in a particular specialist field? Do you use cutting-edge technology in some new and exciting way, or offer some kind of unique service or experience to your clients. Perhaps you specialise in working with a certain type of client (e.g. female entrepreneurs or startup businesses), or maybe you go above and beyond what is normally offered by a bookkeeping business by offering your clients a full suite of end-to-end business advisory services.

My point of difference initially was that I wanted to provide bookkeeping services for Australian Financial Service Licensees (AFSL), rather than to "everybody". Reflecting on it though, another point of difference is providing high-level expertise to clients where we are accessible, responsive, and have a wonderful team with an amazing skill set which clients can really trust. Our "family comes first" philosophy is another thing that differentiates my business from other bookkeeping practices.

## What are your values?

When thinking of a vision for your bookkeeping practice, you will also want to consider the kinds of values that you hold dear. These could be values that you prioritise personally or as a business. Either way, they will have a big impact on the way in which you run your bookkeeping practice, the services you offer, how you engage with your clients, and the staff you attract to work in your business.

For example, is lifelong learning and continuous improvement something that is important to you? Are you someone who accepts failures and sees them as learnings, and who loves to grow and change to find new and better ways to service your clients? If so, this might be something that you want to include in your vision for your business.

Or, do you pride yourself on client communication and going above and beyond to not just meet, but also exceed your clients' expectations every time? Again, this is something that you could incorporate into your vision for your business.

Honesty, trust, integrity, attention to detail, teamwork, respect, and transparency are all examples of other values that you could include in your vision for your bookkeeping business.

## Other tips for finding your vision

When it comes to the perfect vision for your bookkeeping practice, here are a few other things to keep in mind:

- You want something short and concise – two or three sentences at most.

- Your vision should also be written in the present tense, rather than the future tense.

- You want your vision to be fairly broad, as it should be something that will still apply even if you change your service offering or strategy.

- At the same time though, you want it to be bespoke to you and your practice, and specific to what exactly it is that you want to achieve.

- Your vision needs to be authentic and genuine – your customers need to be able to believe your vision, because if they believe in it, then they will believe in you!

My advice would be to spend some time coming up with a few different options for your bookkeeping business's vision. It might take some time and it will evolve over time, but be patient – it's all part of the process. Get creative and try out a few different versions until you settle on one that sums up you and your business.

It might also be worth sharing a couple of your potential visions with your team members, colleagues, or even some of your clients. It can always be useful to get an outside perspective, especially if you're feeling stuck and getting so focused on the finer details that you can't "see the forest for the trees". Getting feedback from a trusted second opinion can help you to clarify the basics – is it clear, is it concise, is it easy to understand, and does it tell them what they need to know about you and your business?

Remember, your vision should be a signpost to help keep you on track to achieving your goals, and will be the thing that gets you from where you are now to what you want and where you're headed. So, you need to make sure that it's clear enough and contains sufficient detail to help you get there!

In the next chapter, we will be looking at defining what you want and where you are heading in more detail. Before reading on, I recommend that you come up with your vision for your bookkeeping practice first, or at least have a few ideas in mind, as we will be building on this in the next chapter.

# Chapter 2: Defining What You Want and Where You Are Heading

Once you've decided on the overarching vision for your bookkeeping business, you will then need to think in more detail about what exactly it is you want, and where it is that your business is heading. For example:

- Are you wanting to offer a comprehensive range of bookkeeping services for your clients, or are you wanting to become more of a specialist and just focus on a few?

- Are you wanting to run a smaller bookkeeping practice where you are very hands on with all of your clients? Or will you eventually scale up and take more of a hands-off client role, with a team of staff to take care of your clients for you?

- Will you be the only bookkeeper in the practice, or will you hire other staff as well? Will these other staff all be bookkeepers, or will you be looking to expand your team with other experts who can diversify the services you offer to your clients? For example, could you hire or partner with an accountant, business advisor, tax specialist, and so on?

- Do you want to offer bookkeeping services in the traditional sense, where you are working directly with your clients? Or do you want to move into things like webinars, online resources, digital downloads, eBooks, and so on that you can sell to a broader range of potential clients?

All of these are questions that you will need to ask yourself when it comes to deciding what you want to get out of your business journey, and where your bookkeeping practice is headed. Whilst your vision will provide you with a good starting point, now is the time to start filling in the gaps by thinking about what that vision will actually look like in practice.

For me, it evolved. Originally, we were going to focus on high-compliance organisations – however, the work was very project-based and I felt I couldn't control the timing of when the next project would come in. This resulted in me changing the business model to more general bookkeeping with specialist services. The consistent bookkeeping allowed me to create a base revenue which was fixed month in and month out. The project work was like the icing on the cake on top of this.

Also, I wanted to do the more complicated work as I enjoy a challenge and I didn't enjoy regular processing work as much. I identified this was the case when I procrastinated with work, not completing it early and finding myself leaving it till last. I also became aware of the fact that time is the most limited resource I have, and so I decided I needed to maximise the hours I spend on what I call "outcome multipliers". Outcome multipliers are tasks that allow me to maximise or multiply the amount of income that I am generating in the same amount of time.

**Practice or company?**

When it comes to what you want and where you're heading, one of the key things you will need to decide is whether you want to operate as a bookkeeping practice, or whether your ultimate goal is to transition to a bookkeeping company.

Opting for a practice structure means that you will be providing bookkeeping services to your clients personally. You might choose to operate as a sole practitioner or as a partnership with another bookkeeper or accountant – both of these could be examples of operation under a practice structure.

By comparison, operating as a company or firm means that rather than providing these to your clients personally, you will be taking more of a hands-off client role. You might be selling services clients can use themselves like training, or you might oversee a team of bookkeepers and other professionals who deliver these services on the business's behalf.

There are definitely advantages to both business models. If you operate as a bookkeeping practice, the advantages include that:

1. You can build a professional reputation for yourself so you become known for your expertise, skills, and the quality of service you provide.

2. You will also likely be more focused on providing a clearly defined set of services.

3. Your services will usually be easier for you to price, as you will be offering the same services to all of your clients, meaning it will also be easier for you to predict cash flow for your business.

However, the disadvantages of this type of structure are that:

1. You can be limited growth-wise. As you only have a limited amount of time and ability to provide your services to your clients, you can become a bottleneck for growth as you can only take on so much work, meaning you will only be able earn up to a certain amount. You also cannot scale client numbers easily. When you are approaching full capacity, it's an indicator to increase your pricing.

2. You may sometimes end up with a tight cash flow, depending on your billing cycle (as you may end up with lots of payments coming in at once, and not many coming in at other times). You have to be working the hours to be invoicing the hours, and if you don't work, you can't invoice. Whilst this can also happen when you work under a company structure, it can sometimes be more frequent when you operate as a practice, as you may be limited by your own time and capacity to take on work and generate additional income.

3. A practice structure is heavily reliant on your expertise, skills, and ability to practise. The business will not be able to keep going if you decide you no longer wish to practise as a bookkeeper, unless you sell your practice on.

On the other hand, the advantages of operating as a company include:

1. There is more opportunity for you to scale your operations. Because you will be offering products and services to your clients rather than your personal time and service, you will not be limited by the amount of time you have available to render services to your clients as you would be with a practice structure, as you will have other team members to complete the work.

2. You are likely to experience more stable cash flow into your business, as you can keep selling the same products and services to new clients, providing you with a recurring income stream. The client won't see a change in your service offering as the work will still be completed.

3. You will be able to offer a broader portfolio of services, as you will have more expertise across different fields available from within the business. This can provide opportunities for you to diversify your revenue stream.

However, the disadvantages are that:

1. It can be more complex to price your products and services, as you will need to factor in more than just your time. For example, you might need to factor in things like software, marketing, staff costs, and the margins you need to make the desired amount of profit.

2. Usually, a company will operate under a company structure, which can be more complex and costly to set up than a sole trader (which is what many practices will operate under).

3. When running a bookkeeping company, you will also need to take on additional responsibilities like staff management. Managing a team of staff and overseeing their delivery of different services can create additional work for you.

These advantages and disadvantages are just some of the things you will need to take into account when deciding which path to pursue. However, there are also a number of other things that you will need to consider when deciding whether a practice or company structure is the right choice for you. For example, if you love being hands on and working directly with your clients, you might prefer to stay operating as a bookkeeping practice. However, if your goal is to earn more money whilst taking more of a hands-off role and focusing more on high-level tasks rather than the day-to-day ones, you might prefer to transition to a company structure.

Personally, for many years, I ran my own bookkeeping practice. More recently though, I have transitioned into running a company. For me, the vision was freedom. Working with clients had created the opposite of that, as I had to deliver client work to manage clients' expectations, which was one of the reasons why I decided to transition to a company to achieve my vision of freedom and flexibility.

The decision between running a practice or a company largely comes down to personal preference, and what exactly it is you want to get out of running your own business. You will also need to think about what happens in future, if you ever decide to sell your business. On exit, bookkeeping companies in Australia can sell for anywhere from $0.90–1.40 for every dollar of revenue, whereas bookkeeping practices command the lower side of the range. It really is dependent on whether someone can step into the business easily. This is another thing to keep in mind, as you are building an asset that you can sell later on.

It is completely fine if you feel that running a bookkeeping practice is the best choice for you, and it is equally okay if you want to make the move to running your own company. The main thing is to make sure that you are achieving your "why" – because if you are not achieving what you ultimately want, what is the point in doing it?

For me, the big realisation was that I needed to create freedom with time, as I wanted to start a family. By not setting my business up to scale from the outset, I had actually reduced my freedom significantly, as I was constantly having to strive to earn x amount of money. My ability to earn was also restricted by my time, as time is a limited resource because you can only work so many hours. Once I was able to recognise that I was not achieving my "why" – freedom – I was able to pivot, and reassess my business model to put it back on track in order to achieve my "why".

So, keep your "why" or your end goal in mind and build your plan around that. Think about what it is you need to do to get from where you are now to where you want to be, and come up with a list of action steps or things you can do to help you get there.

Every time you do something, ask yourself: is this bringing me closer to achieving my "why"? If not, ask yourself why not, and think about what you can change about that thing to ensure you're more on track to creating your vision.

## Deciding what you'll do – know your strengths

Once you've decided where you want to take your business and what kind of structure you intend to operate under, the other thing you'll need to do is decide exactly what kinds of products or services you will be offering. When making this decision, my advice would be to know and focus on your strengths.

Whilst it is important to stretch yourself and continually grow and change, there are also times when it is important to know your strengths, whilst also recognising that some things are better done by others.

For your bookkeeping business to be a success, you should define your product and service offering early. Your product and service offering should align with your strengths, or where you are the most skilled or have the most expertise. Concentrating on these areas will enable you to provide your clients with the highest quality of service, as opposed to trying to focus on too many areas (including those that you might not be that great at!) just to offer as many services as possible.

Doing this will also allow you to maximise your return on your hours. By focusing on higher-level tasks or "multiplier" tasks, and delegating those that are less valuable to your business as they generate less revenue, you will be well placed to maximise your income. Do this, and watch your income explode!

You might have heard the expression "jack of all trades, master of none" – and the same applies in this situation. It is better for you to be really, really great at a few key services and position yourself as an expert in these areas and provide your clients with a really high-quality service than to offer lots of different services of a poorer quality.

For example, if bookkeeping is your strength, there is no harm in focusing your professional practice or company on this. However, if you decide to start offering lots of other business advisory services just because that's what your competitors are doing, despite having no skills or experience in this area, you might be doing more harm to your business than good if you attempt to take this on. In saying that, I strongly believe you need to know where to get the answer, and that you don't necessarily need to have all the answers yourself. If you choose to offer services which are not in your area of expertise, just ensure you have someone who can guide you to meet client expectations.

I've definitely been caught out by this myself. In the earlier years of running my own business, I was trying to do everything and be everything to everyone! I started out being very generalist, though over time, I fine-tuned the service offering to become more focused on specific revenue streams (or the things that made me money, as opposed to the things that did not). The game changer was also when I started delegating lower-level tasks to someone else, as this way I was able to focus more on the higher-level tasks that commanded my personal attention and expertise. I also started to think strategically about how I could make more by doing less, and found ways to multiply my growth through "multiplier" tasks that would continue to generate revenue.

By all means, there is no reason why you can't continue adding new product and service offerings to your practice or company. However, it is important that you have the skills, knowledge, and experience in these areas to be able to do justice to them and provide your clients with the quality of service that they deserve. If not, there is always the option for you to take on someone else – be it an employee or contractor – who does have these skills, who can then offer these kinds of services to your clients. Alternatively, you can find a mentor to advise how to deliver the services.

# Chapter 3: Identifying and Marketing to Your Ideal Client

Identifying your ideal client is one of the most important things you will need to do when setting up your bookkeeping business, as you will be focusing on these types of clients when it comes to how you market and grow your business. Remember, you are not here to appeal to cost-focused clients who are looking for the lowest price – you are here to offer high-quality bookkeeping services to clients who are on the same wavelength as you, and who know your worth and the value you can create for their business.

Whilst you may need to take on anything and everything to begin with, especially during the first few years of running your business, there will come a time when you can afford to become more choosy. This will mean you can focus solely on these ideal clients who are an ideal fit for you and your business, and weed out clients who are not a fit. Usually, this will be at around the $250k mark.

This milestone is an important one in your business journey, as it represents one of the major decision points where you will need to make a choice that will influence the course that your business will take overall. Do you carry on being a jack of all trades, or do you carve out a really specific niche where you provide a particular kind of expertise to a specialised type of client? This is where the part about identifying and marketing to your ideal client comes in.

## The importance of knowing your ideal client persona

When we talk about your "ideal" client, we are basically talking about the type of person that would be the best possible fit for you and the services you offer. Your ideal client will be someone who knows your worth and who is prepared to pay you for the value that you create for them. They will also align with your vision and values, and will help you to move closer towards achieving your "why".

To ensure that you are best placed to be able to target your ideal client, it is important that you are very clear about what your ideal client actually looks like. This will ensure that you are able to design and implement closely tailored targeted marketing strategies that will help you get your business and services in front of these types of ideal clients with whom you want to work.

Some of the other benefits of knowing who your target customer actually is include:

- It helps you to target customers who are likely to be interested in your product or service.

- It helps you to focus on offering specific services and working with a certain group of clients who will bring you closer to achieving your "why".

- It allows you to be more specific and intentional with your marketing.

- It provides you with more insights into your ideal clients' wants, needs, and preferences, meaning you can then fine-tune your service offering to align with these things.

- It saves you time and money in the long run, as you won't be investing in marketing techniques that are unlikely to reach your ideal customer.

**Coming up with a persona**

To define what your ideal client looks like, it's advisable to come up with an ideal client profile or persona that, in essence, sets out the characteristics or requirements that your ideal client will have. This will include things like their wants, needs, preferences, what they value, what problems they have, and what they want to get out of your services – all of which will help to ensure you are addressing your ideal client and their needs when it comes to how your market yourself as a business.

Here are some things that you might include in your ideal client persona:

- Demographics, such as:

  o What age group are they in? (For example, are you targeting young people in their twenties, young professionals in their twenties and thirties, businesswomen in their forties and fifties, and so on?)

  o What gender are they? (For example, are they men, women, or both? Are you targeting female entrepreneurs and small business owners or male "tradies", for instance?)

  o What area do they live in? (For example, are you only targeting clients in your local area and surrounds or clients from all over the world by offering your services online?)

o What kind of income do they earn? (For example, do you want to work with "average" income earners, or people who generate a significant amount of income?)

o What type of job do they do or what kind of business do they run? (For example, will you be working with clients who run their own businesses, or who work in a particular field or industry? If they are running their own business, what kinds of products and services do they offer, and what industry do they operate in?)

o What struggles or problems are they having at present? (For example, are they struggling to grow their businesses? Are they struggling to keep on top of their cashflow? Are they stumped about where to start when it comes to bookkeeping for their business?)

o What would make their life easier? (For example, do they want an end-to-end, all-inclusive solution? Or are they wanting more one-off, ad hoc support when an issue arises? What specific services would add value for them and make their lives easier?)

o What kinds of services are they looking for? (For example, do they need help with tax requirements? Preparing financial reports? Expense tracking? Payroll? Invoice processing? Cash flow forecasting? Are they wanting your "average" bookkeeping services, or are they wanting someone who can take on more of a business advisory role?)

o What kinds of things do they like or value? (For example, do they value convenience and 24/7 online access? Do they want fast turnaround times? Do they want to deal with you in person, over the phone, via email, or over Zoom? Do they like packages and bundles or one-off services?)

o What are their needs and requirements? (For example, do they need someone who can work with them after hours? Do they need someone who can come to their office and work with them in person? Do they need your help on specific days or at specific times? Are there any specific requirements they have that relate to the type of business they run or the industry in which they operate?)

o What is their budget for your services? (For example, do they have a lot of money to invest in a good bookkeeping service, or would they be more interested in a bundle or package deal that offers them a discount on key services?)

All of these questions will help you to develop a clear picture of who your ideal client is and what their wants, needs, and requirements are. This will guide you in shaping a tailored service offering that aligns with what your ideal clients are looking for in a bookkeeping practice.

**How do you know who your ideal clients are?**

By working your way through the above questions and creating a profile or persona for what your ideal client looks like, you should be able to develop a better idea of who your ideal clients are. However, there are several other sources of information that you can consult to find out more about who your ideal clients might be.

For example, you might look at the types of clients your business has already been servicing and, from there, narrow it down to focus on one or two specific types. Up until now, you might have serviced "everybody" with a range of general bookkeeping services. However, you might decide that you want to hone in on female entrepreneurs and business owners who are looking for a one-stop-shop for all of their bookkeeping needs. This way, you are filtering out all of the other clients who do not fit your ideal client persona, who may be looking for ad hoc, one-off services, to instead focus on your ideal clients and service them through all-inclusive bookkeeping bundles. Likewise, you might have previously been servicing both individual clients and business clients, but decide that you only want to serve business clients from now on. Therefore, you could decide to move out all of your smaller individual clients and instead focus on the business clients to whom you want to offer your services.

In addition to your current client base, other sources of information could be your website's Google Analytics, social media analytics, or email newsletter analytics. All of these will enable you to identify the demographics and types of clients who you are engaging with, so you can then narrow these down to find your ideal persona.

### How many ideal client personas can you have?

My advice would be to narrow down to between one and three ideal client personas. I'd advise against having any more than three ideal client personas, otherwise you will lack clarity and find it hard to focus on each persona and target them effectively.

For example, if you decide you want to focus on female entrepreneurs who are looking for an end-to-end bookkeeping service, it would be fairly easy for you to tailor your marketing strategy to strategically target this group as your ideal client. However, if you then decide you also want to target trades, you are taking away a bit of the marketing focus from the first ideal client that you defined. This is definitely still doable, as you could then create a second targeted marketing profile and strategy to target the second ideal client type that you defined. If you then decide though that you also want to specialise in payroll for all kinds of businesses, you are then diluting your focus even further, as you will be offering this service to all kinds of businesses – not just the two niches that you initially set out to target: meaning you will have to target marketing at female entrepreneurs, trades, and now payroll for all business types. Also, it can be more difficult (though not impossible) to design, implement, and maintain three different targeted marketing strategies: full bookkeeping for both female entrepreneurs and trades and payroll for all business types.

Not only that, but focusing on too many ideal client types can dilute your brand. For example, if you wanted to focus on female entrepreneurs, you could make this your brand, and position yourself as a dedicated bookkeeper for women who run their own small businesses who are looking for a comprehensive bookkeeping service. Over time, you would likely become known as an expert in this field, and may even become a go-to for female entrepreneurs and businesswomen in your local area who are looking for this kind of service. By comparison though, if you offer services for female entrepreneurs, trades, and payroll, you are not really defining yourself as a specialist in one particular niche. Therefore, you are likely to become known more as a "jack of all trades" (or jill of all trades!), rather than someone who has really honed their skills and become an expert in a particular niche.

Again, this will really depend on what your "why" is and what your goals are for your business. Some bookkeepers want to service everybody, and maybe this is the right choice for you. Personally though, I have found it is better to narrow down and focus on one or two ideal client types, otherwise it makes it harder to find and connect with the types of clients you really want to deal with if you are positioning yourself as the type of bookkeeper who services "everybody".

For me, I decided that business bookkeeping was a service that we wanted to specialise in. However, I decided to hone this down even further to reflect my areas of interest and expertise, the types of clients that I enjoyed working with the most, and the types of businesses where I felt I could add the most value. In the end, I decided that my ideal client was going to be Australian Financial Services (AFSL) holders and other established high-compliance businesses with an annual turnover of up to $20 million. This allowed me to focus my strategy on these kinds of customers who are looking for meticulous financial administration, improved reporting capabilities, accurate numbers, and help with achieving ongoing compliance. In my case, the needs and requirements of my target clients aligned with my own personal strengths and areas of expertise as an accountant and bookkeeper, which meant it made sense for me to specialise in this area.

## How to strategically target your ideal client through targeted marketing

Once you have identified your ideal client type, you will know more about who you actually want to be directing your marketing at. By understanding your target audience, you will be able to develop marketing strategies that will target these types of people more efficiently and effectively. As a result, you will be better informed about how to market to your ideal customer specifically.

This process of targeting a particular type of customer specifically through marketing is known as "targeted marketing". Through targeted marketing, we are able to develop a marketing strategy that is highly personalised and closely tailored to the specific wants, needs, and requirements of our ideal clients. Rather than advertising our services in a broader, more general way to "everybody", we instead market ourselves in a way that appeals to what our ideal clients are actually looking for. This increases the effectiveness and efficiency of our marketing efforts, as we are only advertising our services to clients who are likely to be interested in them. This means that we are essentially only targeting those ideal clients for whom our services are the best fit.

With targeted marketing, there are many different ways in which you can focus on specific demographics or other characteristics. For example, you could segment your targeted marketing strategies based on things such as:

- Age
- Gender
- Income level
- Country

- State, city, or suburb
- Socioeconomic status
- Values
- Beliefs
- Interests
- Preferences

The better-defined your ideal client persona is, the easier it will be for you to target them via marketing that appeals directly to their wants, needs, and specific requirements. All of these things make your ideal clients more likely to choose your business to help them with all of their bookkeeping needs, because through your targeted marketing efforts, you are showing them how your services can solve their problems and meet their specific needs.

For example, if you are positioning yourself as a specialist in payroll, your marketing could revolve around something like "Payroll stressing you out? Let us take care of them for you!" or "Your one-stop payroll shop". This way, you are immediately telling your clients what it is you offer and how you can solve their problems. Problem? They're stressed about payroll. Solution? You will take care of their payroll for them. This is providing your ideal client with a direct link between their problem and the solution you are offering.

As another example, going back to our previous example where we talked about deciding to specialise in female entrepreneurs and small business owners, you might start publishing content and thought leadership pieces on issues relevant to small businesses. In doing so, you are educating your target customers about some of the common issues they might be experiencing. You could also include a call to action or link around how your business can help them to solve those issues.

## Targeted marketing approaches

There are many different marketing methods that can be optimised for targeted marketing, ranging from emails, social media, and SMS marketing to content marketing and paid advertising through Google Ads. The best targeting marketing methods for your bookkeeping services will largely be determined by the type of client you are targeting, along with other factors such as your marketing budget and business goals.

When it comes to targeted marketing, I'd also suggest investing in paid ads targeted to your specific demographic. This may be out of budget in the early days of running your business. However, by the time you hit the $250–500k mark (which is the point when you're likely to start honing in on servicing your ideal client), targeted paid ads on social media can be a cost-effective way for you to get in front of as many eyeballs as possible from within your defined target market.

For example, if you are targeting female entrepreneurs in their forties and fifties, you would want to do some research to find out which social media platforms are used the most by women in this cohort. You would then want to set up targeted social media advertisements or paid posts to ensure they are being shown to women in their forties and fifties who are interested in entrepreneurship or who run their own businesses.

The value of networking and word-of-mouth referrals also cannot be underestimated. Going back to the previous example where you decide to target women in business, you might join some local networking groups designed for women in business. If you service clients remotely, you could also join one of the many online communities for female entrepreneurs, which could connect you with any number of new clients who may be looking for your services. Also, as you begin to build up your client base of clients within your ideal niche, you will often find that your existing clients pass your details on to their friends or colleagues, which can be another fantastic way to connect with more of your ideal clients.

Finally, look for opportunities to build partnerships with other businesses who service your ideal clients. Quite often, you will find that they will be more than happy to pass on your details to any of their own clients who might be looking for bookkeeping services!

# Chapter 4: Launching Your Bookkeeping Business

## Setting up the basics

Once you've decided on your vision and direction, it's time to think about launching your bookkeeping business. There's lots to do before you can launch though! You will need to:

- Create a business plan: A business plan sets out your goals for your business and how you intend to go about achieving them.

When most people think of business plans, they tend to think of massive multi-page documents with tables and graphs and all sorts. When you're first starting out though, there's no need to go into this level of detail - just one or two pages covering the basics will suffice. You can then continue to expand on this as you build your bookkeeping business.

Your business plan should include things like your vision, value proposition, target market, competitors, goals and targets, and major milestones. Much of this builds upon what we were discussing in the first couple of chapters, so if you have already come up with your vision and have an idea about where you want to go with your business, you should have a lot of this information ready to go.

In your business plan, you will also want to include a brief overview of how you plan to go about marketing your business.

- Decide on your business structure: When you start setting up your bookkeeping business, you will also need to decide whether you plan on operating as a sole trader or partnership or operating under a company structure.

As we touched on previously, if your goal is to operate as a smaller practice, setting up as a sole trader may be fine. However, if your goal is to set up as a larger practice or company, you might find that a company structure will work better for you. Each type of business structure comes with its own advantages and disadvantages, which you will need to take into account when deciding which will be best for your bookkeeping business.

For example, a sole trader structure is the simplest and most cost effective to set up. As a sole trader, you and your business will be seen as a single entity from a legal point of view. This means that you will be responsible for all aspects of your business, giving you full control over the business and assets. When operating as a sole trader, there are less reporting requirements than with other types of business structures. However, sole traders have unlimited liability for their business, meaning that your personal assets (such as your house, car, and own savings) could be at risk if things go wrong.

A partnership structure (where you set up a practice with one or more other bookkeepers, an accountant, or other finance and business professionals) is another option that is similar to a sole trader structure, in that it can be easier and less complex to set up than a company. There are three different partnership structures: a general partnership, where all of the partners are equally responsible for the business and have unlimited liability for its debts and obligations; a limited partnership, where the liability of some of the partners will be limited to the amount of money they put into the business, while some of the others have unlimited liability; or an incorporated limited partnership, where all of the partners have limited liability for the business's debts, with the exception of one partner who assumes unlimited liability.

By comparison, when you opt to set up under a company structure, your business will be established as a completely separate legal entity. This means that you will not be personally liable for any debts incurred by the company if things do go wrong (there a few exceptions as a director is held liable for unpaid superannuation, etc). However, the drawback with this type of business structure is that it can be more complex and costly to set up. Companies also have more reporting requirements than sole traders do.

- Get an Australian Business Number (ABN): In Australia, anyone running a business needs to register for an ABN, which is a unique 11-digit number that is used to identify you and your business.

If you are going to be setting up as a company, you will need to apply for an Australian Company Number (ACN), which is a unique 9-digit identifier for your company.

If you are going to be acting as the director of your company, you will also need to get a director ID, which is a unique 15-digit number used to identify company directors. Whilst previously this was not a prerequisite, as of 2023 the Corporations Act 2001 now requires all company directors to apply for a director ID before they are able to act as the director of a company.

- Pick a business name: You will also need to decide on a business name. This is a requirement for businesses that will be operating under a company structure.

  If you are going to be operating as a sole trader and plan to open a small bookkeeping practice under your own name (for example, John Smith), you will not need to register an additional business name. However, you will need to register a business name if you want to add the word "bookkeeping" or anything else to your business name (for example, John Smith Bookkeeping rather than just John Smith).

- Make sure you have a tax file number (TFN): If you are going to be operating as a sole trader, chances are you already have a TFN. This will be the same as the TFN you use to file your own personal tax returns.

However, if you are going to be setting up as a company, you will need to apply for a new TFN. This is because companies are required to have their own tax file numbers which are separate to those of their directors.

- Register your company: If you are going to be setting up as a sole trader, you can skip this step. However, if you plan to set up as a company, you will need to register your company with the ASIC.

- Create a business bank account: If you are going to be operating as a sole trader, it is not mandatory to set up a business bank account. Because you and your business are considered to be one and the same from a legal point of view, you are able to use your personal bank account for business banking if you wish. However, my advice would still be to set up a separate account for your bookkeeping business, as it makes things so much easier come tax time when you need to separate out your personal and business income and expenses.

  If you are setting up as a company, it is recommended that you have a separate bank account for your business – you can get yourself into a lot of trouble when you use a personal bank account for business purposes.

- Get insured: You should also get business insurance to ensure you are protected if anything goes wrong with your business.

  As a bookkeeper, the main type of insurance you will need is professional indemnity insurance, which is a type of liability insurance that provides cover in the event someone makes a claim against you for any kind of mistake, wrongdoing, error or omission, or breach of professional duty. An example could be if you made a mistake with your client's bookkeeping that ended up costing them a lot of money. Holding professional indemnity insurance would cover you for the financial consequences of such a claim, including both legal costs and damages payable.

Some of the other types of insurance you may want to consider include:

o Public liability insurance (which will protect you if a customer or other member of the public is injured or their property is damaged as a result of your business activities)

o Business insurance (which will cover you for damage to your building and contents or interruptions to your business)

o Cyber liability insurance (which will protect you in the event of a cyberattack or privacy breach)

o Directors' and officers' insurance (which will protect you against any claims made against you personally as a company director)

**Marketing your business**

Once you've got all the technical formalities out of the way, the only thing left to do is to start marketing your business. That means getting your business out in front of as many potential customers from your target market as possible, and doing what you can to convert them into paying clients.

When you think "marketing", things like websites and social media profiles are probably some of the first things that come to mind. In actual fact though, word-of-mouth and client referrals are actually two of the most effective marketing techniques for bookkeepers!

If you have already been working as a bookkeeper, the best thing you can do is to market yourself within your existing network. Speak to other bookkeepers, accountants, and other business and financial professionals from within your network. Perhaps they know of someone who is looking for a particular service that they do not offer that they want to refer on!

You can even network with others from within your own personal and professional networks who perhaps don't work within the finance industry, but whose own clients could be looking for these kinds of services. For example, maybe you know somebody who works as a business coach, a mortgage broker, or a marketing consultant. Perhaps they are looking to partner with a bookkeeping practice to whom they can refer their clients!

The key is to strategically target your own network. Think of people who have your target clients as their own clients. Then, see how you can leverage the connection you have with that person to help them find new ways to add value for their clients – for example, by referring them on to your business for all their bookkeeping needs. You will quickly start to notice the "multiplier effect", as the more people refer their clients to you, the more potential clients you will have reaching out.

When it comes to more conventional marketing, it definitely has its place. Personally, I would advise against spending too much on marketing to start with. When I first started out, I spent a truckload on all kinds of marketing activities that ultimately ended up being a waste of time and money. I just did it because I thought I had to but in the end all that money spent on marketing ended up doing little to help my business.

What I would say is to start with a basic website. I'd recommend outsourcing this if you can, though if you are restricted by cash, you can build one yourself. You definitely don't need a full elaborate website and branding package to start. In fact, there are plenty of free or very affordable website developers online that will allow you to get up and running for a low investment. Your website only needs to be something basic so that if potential clients Google your name, they can find you online. This goes a long way in increasing your credibility, particularly if you are just starting out.

You could also set up some basic social media profiles for your business if you want to. However, this is not a must-have and is something that you can always work on later. Remember, you can always build up to different types of marketing activities later; for the moment you only really need the absolute basics to get started.

### Post launch

Once you're all set up legally and have started marketing yourself to potential clients, it's time to launch!

The biggest piece of advice I could give to any new business owner is to not get disheartened, particularly if you don't have customers knocking on your door from day one. It's the same with any new business, including bookkeeping businesses. It takes time to build up a client base, but with perseverance and great work, it is definitely doable! Just keep working at it and you'll get there.

The other thing I would say is to know that you will make mistakes along the way. There will be things that you look back on later and think, why did I do that? I definitely did, when I realised all the original marketing activity I'd invested in when setting up my business ended up being a waste of time and money. The important thing though is to see these mistakes not as failures, but as lessons that you can learn from. You might do something which is a huge success, so you decide you'll definitely do that again in future. Other times, you might do something and it just doesn't work out. But if that happens, you can learn from it and then have another go.

Finally, remember that you are your word. What I mean by that is that you always need to do what you say you are going to do. Don't go making all these big promises to your clients and then fail to deliver (e.g. saying "I'll get this done for you tomorrow!" and then days go by without them hearing anything from you), as this will give you a reputation for being unreliable.

Sure, things happen, but if you realise you're not going to be able to deliver what you promised, be transparent with your client. Communicate this to them early, explain what has happened, and recommit to a new date. Your clients will understand if something comes up and you can't do what you initially promised – as long as you are honest and upfront with them about it.

By doing this, you will be able to manage your clients' expectations and build a reputation for yourself as being an honest, trustworthy, and reliable bookkeeping professional that they can depend on. Keep it up, and you will soon be building strong relationships with your clients. With time, your clients will start to see you as their go-to for all their bookkeeping needs, and will continue to refer you to all their friends and colleagues, drumming up more business for you along the way.

# Section 2: Pricing
# Chapter 5: Pricing Strategies for Success

Pricing is another thing that you will need to continuously visit and revisit throughout your journey of growing your bookkeeping practice. When you first start out, you may find that you charge lower prices to attract as many new clients and as much business as you can. As you grow your business though, you will have more scope to revisit your pricing and increase your fees accordingly – particularly when you hit the $250k mark, this is when you will be able to afford to be more choosy about who you do and don't take on as a client.

As the owner of a successful bookkeeping business, it is important that you are charging your clients at a rate that is commensurate with your skills and experience, as well as the value that you offer to your customers. You don't want to charge too little for your services, as then you are selling yourself short by not recognising the value and expertise you can offer your clients and you will get burnt out. By not charging your clients what you are worth, you are missing out on an opportunity to make a profit which, in turn, can have an impact on the overall success of your bookkeeping practice. On the other hand though, you also don't want to charge too much as, depending on the type of clients you want to work with, you might price yourself out of the market – particularly if they can get the same value at a more affordable price elsewhere.

It's all about striking a fine balance between not charging too much but not charging too little either. For this reason, it's important to do your research and find out what your competitors are charging to establish what the going rate is for bookkeeping practices that offer a similar value proposition to you. You may also need to do some soul searching to find out what it really is that you offer which makes you stand out from the rest, and why clients should choose you over all the other bookkeepers out there. Once you know what your value proposition is and recognise the value you can add to your clients' lives and businesses, you will likely feel more confident charging accordingly.

**Pricing strategies for bookkeeping practices**
When it comes to pricing the services that you offer at your bookkeeping practice, there are a few approaches you can take. The best pricing strategy for you will be largely determined by things like the products or services you offer, your business size, your business goals, the needs and wants of your clients, and your experience level. As a general guide though, here are some common pricing strategies that might be used by bookkeeping practices:

- Hourly rate: This pricing strategy is commonly used by bookkeeping practices, and is where you charge your clients a fixed hourly rate based on the amount of time it takes you to complete a particular task. For example, if you charge $85 an hour and you file a BAS return which takes you two hours, you would then charge the client $170.

- Fixed price: This pricing strategy is where you charge a fixed price for a particular project, product, or service.

It may also be referred to as charging by the service. An example could be if you charge a flat fee to file a basic BAS return. Likewise, if you offer products to your clients (e.g. training packages or eBooks), you would sell these at a fixed price.

- Ongoing fixed price or recurring revenue: You could also operate under a subscription model. This is similar to the fixed price model, as you will be charging your clients the same price each time in exchange for a particular service. The difference is that this is billed to them on a regular recurring basis (e.g. weekly or monthly), rather than as a one-off. For example, you could bill under a fixed rate recurring revenue model for basic bookkeeping tasks that you complete every week for your clients which take the same amount of time to complete each time.

- Retainer rates: This is a variation of the fixed pricing strategy. When you service clients on retainer, you are charging them a fixed monthly rate that provides them with a certain amount of your time for that month. The way I package this is that they must pay a retainer so that a certain number of hours are allocated to the client. You or your team member have limited hours, and you need to allocate time to the specific client. If anything else comes up, this is charged as extra for the period.

For example, if your hourly rate is $80, you might offer monthly retainer packages for $800 for ten hours of your time, $1,600 for twenty hours of your time, $3,200 for forty hours of your time, and so on. You might choose a volume discounts to incentive potential clients buy larger packages, this might looks like $800 for ten hours of your time, $1,500 for twenty hours, or $2,900 for forty hours, then you could charge additional hours at your regular hourly rate on top of this if your client needs more of your time.

- Value-based: This pricing strategy is where you are charging for the value that your products or services provide to your clients, rather than necessarily the time or effort it takes you to complete each task. This approach is based more on the perceived worth or value that your services have to your clients, and the assumption that clients will be willing to pay more for services that are of value to them. Basically, you will be setting your prices based on how much you think your clients will be willing to pay to solve a particular problem, or how much they are willing to pay for the value you can offer to them. This is great, as you can improve how you deliver services so you do it faster and quicker, and increase your gross profit.

For example, if you are a very experienced bookkeeper who has been running your own bookkeeping company for many years, you might offer training and consulting services. You might offer these services at a higher price point than your competitors, however, your clients will be prepared to pay this because you have already walked the path before them, and know what works and doesn't work. Therefore, the value and firsthand experience that you have is of great value to them, meaning they will be prepared to pay more for this.

- Bundling: Another option is to bundle your services, which is where you package together two or more of your services in one bundle and charge your clients a single fixed price for them. This may also be referred to as "productising your services".

Generally speaking, you will have a few different packages or bundles that include different services. For example, you might have one package that offers a company bookkeeping and four BAS for a fixed monthly cost. Likewise, you might have one that offers Xero subscription and monthly bank reconciliations for a fixed monthly cost. You might have another that is more comprehensive and which offers things like bank reconciliations, payroll, accounts payable and receivable, invoicing, monthly or quarterly financial statements, and bank reconciliations all in one bundle, and so on.

You could also package your services based on different levels of service – for example, a bronze package that has a few basic inclusions, a silver package that has some additional inclusions on top of this, a gold package with even more inclusions, and a platinum package that has a range of inclusions to offer a more comprehensive solution. Alternatively, you could tailor custom packages for clients who are looking for a specific combination of services.

Bundling has the advantage of offering simplicity. For clients who are unsure what services they need or who are looking for a more comprehensive, all-in-one solution, bundling is likely to be a big drawcard for them. It also allows you to maximise your profits by selling more services to your clients, as the perceived convenience and ease will make them more likely to purchase more services in one package deal.

- Adding a premium: Sometimes, you might charge a premium or surcharge on top of your regular fees for certain tasks. An example could be if you were completing bookkeeping for a high-compliance client, which requires a greater understanding than standard bookkeeping for regular clients, in which case you might charge an additional fee to account for the added complexity.

  You might also charge a higher rate for after-hours requests, last-minute requests, works that are out of scope, or for more "premium" services based on your personal expertise (for example, if you offer consulting or training services for other bookkeepers).

  You might even charge a higher rate if there's certain services that you technically offer but which you do not enjoy or are trying to discourage clients from engaging you to complete. For example, you might have previously completed clean-up jobs for $500. However, if you wanted to get away from clean-up work, you might decide to more than double your prices and charge $1,000 for this instead.

- One-off services: You could also offer one-off services. One thing we do is a compliance health check package for onboarding, where we go through and check all regulatory addresses, contacts, business name registrations, and so on for the client. These one-off services would be charged at a fixed price.

Each pricing strategy has pros and cons, which you will need to take into account when working out which strategy will work best for you and your business.

For example, charging at an hourly rate can sometimes be better for bookkeeping practices that are just starting out or new bookkeepers who do not have much experience, as clients are able to pay for your services by the hour. This can give them confidence in working with a newer or less experienced bookkeeper, as they are not locked into a project-based contract or retainer where they have to commit to a certain number of hours upfront for a significant fee. Instead, they can pay by the hour. Hourly pricing can also make it easier for new bookkeepers to determine the right price point, based on what their competitors who charge an hourly rate are charging. In addition, this type of pricing can offer some flexibility, as you can increase your hourly rate as you become more experienced. I would also recommend that you bill in advance for a certain number of hours as a package, as this will help you to ensure you get paid on time and are paid adequately for the service you are providing.

However, this type of pricing does have some drawbacks. As we mentioned previously, this pricing strategy does not provide you with any kind of incentive or motivation to become more efficient at what you do, as if you complete tasks faster, you will have to charge your clients less for them (unless you up your hourly rate to compensate for this). With that said, you could only increase your hourly rate up to a certain point before people start seeing it as "too expensive" (for example, you may get a limited number of clients if you charge $500 an hour for bookkeeping).

When you work on an hourly rate, your ability to grow and generate a profit is also capped by your time, as you only have so many hours in the day, and therefore only a finite amount of time within which you can render services to your clients. This means you can only earn up to a certain maximum, based on the number of hours that you work. Furthermore, bookkeepers who charge an hourly rate may also feel pressure to offer the cheapest price or price match their competitors (e.g. "Bookkeeper B charges $40 an hour, but you charge $60. Can you match their price?").

By comparison, charging by the project or for the value you are offering to your clients provides you with the uncapped potential to earn and make a profit. Because you are charging for the end result and the value you are able to create for your clients, you are not restricted by the number of hours you are able to charge for, meaning the growth opportunities are endless. The biggest advantage of this pricing strategy is that you can start getting paid what you're worth, rather than just the amount of time it takes you to complete a particular task. It can also be easier for you to raise your rates, as your clients will be less likely to question why your rates are increasing, because they will be able to recognise and appreciate the value that you are creating for their business.

The main drawback with this type of pricing is that it can be more challenging to identify the right price point for your business, particularly when you are just starting out. It may also be more difficult for new bookkeepers and less established bookkeeping practices to justify charging under a value-based model, however, it is not impossible. Finally, it can take some trial and error to get your pricing right, meaning you may end up undercharging or overcharging in the meantime until you strike the perfect balance and get your pricing just right.

When I first started out, we started on fixed pricing, but clients were slow to pay, meaning I would sometimes end up 8–12 weeks behind on payments. I flipped this by getting most clients to pay in advance and it was a game changer. I also know that if they have not paid, I am taking a risk if we still service the client as it may result in non-payment.

Another thing which has become apparent is that often cost-conscious clients are a lot more work than clients who see the value in your services. These clients will happily pay for your services as they see your value, and often don't question pricing because they value what you bring to the table. This, however, comes down to knowing your ideal client.

**How to find the right price point**
Whatever pricing strategy you decide to go with, you will need to spend some time doing your research to find the right price point for your services.

Doing competitor research is a great way to find out what other bookkeeping practices are charging for the same services. Otherwise, here are my pricing recommendations for some common bookkeeping services that you are likely to offer at your business.

- Bookkeeping services: $65 - 135 per hour
- Payroll services: $85 - 150 per hour

- BAS lodgement: $198 - 850 (depending if you are reviewing what is in the file and reworking it or not)
- One-off rectification: $90 - 150 per hour (this is slightly higher as they are paying for expertise)
- Set up a new file where you are bringing over historical data: minimum of $550
- Brand new file set-up: $150
- Accounts receivable is a tricky one: Price varies (as it often takes a lot of time, so you may like to charge for this separately and the client can choose to add this on when required)

Note: The above price list reflects Australian pricing as of April 2025.

Remember, the right price point for your bookkeeping business will very much be determined by your expertise and skill level. If you are an entry-level bookkeeper who has not been practising for long, you will likely find that you charge at the lower end of the scale to begin with. By comparison, when you are more experienced, you will be able to demand higher rates for your expertise as there is not as much pressure on your cashflow. This is because you would be heading towards maximising your time, meaning you can start moving your pricing upwards. Although there is a risk of losing clients, you will still have enough work to cover your personal needs if that happens. Remember too that the increased price for the other clients will likely cover the clients that leave, so you will be working less for more.

Setting your price also means setting clients' expectations, which will also influence the type of client you will attract.

**Pricing mistakes to avoid**

There are a few common mistakes that bookkeepers tend to make when pricing up their services. It is worth being aware of these, to help you be mindful to not fall into the same traps or pitfalls when developing the pricing strategy for your own bookkeeping practice:

- Charging by the hour: One of the most common is charging by the hour. Whilst this is certainly one way in which you can price your services, if your main goal is to generate wealth and create financial freedom, you could be severely limiting yourself.

  For one thing, charging an hourly rate only allows you to charge for the amount of time it actually takes you to complete the work. This doesn't take into account other factors, such as your expertise and skill level, or the value you are creating for your clients by offering your services to them, which can go far beyond a $65 hourly rate, for example. In charging by the hour, you are essentially turning your work into a commodity, as you are getting paid for time spent rather than the outcome you create. This ties into the whole "know your value" piece that we were talking about earlier, because your expertise is worth more than an hourly rate.

  Further, there is no motivation for you to work as efficiently as possible when you are charging by the hour, as you will only be able to charge the client for the amount of hours you actually work. For example, when you're starting out, it might take you a certain number of hours for a clean-up job, but when you have a bit more experience under your belt, you might be able to get this done in half the time. However, there is no advantage to becoming more efficient in this case as you'll be charging the client for less time, and therefore making less money.

The only option here to increase your profit would be to charge a higher hourly rate. However, with this type of pricing, you are also more likely to attract clients who are more focused on cost than the value you provide. This means that if you make your hourly rate too high, you risk clients telling you "that's too much" – particularly if you used to charge them a much lower rate in the past. By the same token, you wouldn't be able to bill your clients for more hours at the same rate, as they would then be questioning why a task that used to take you two hours to complete now takes you four hours to complete, for instance.

- Not factoring in all their costs: Another mistake that is commonly made by bookkeeping practices, especially those that are just starting out, is failing to factor in all of their costs to the pricing equation.

For example, new bookkeepers or bookkeeping practices that are just starting out might feel pressured to beat their competitors' prices in order to attract new clients and new business (for example, by offering very cheap rates or an offer that is "too good to refuse"). In doing this though, they might be setting prices that are too low and which do not cover all of their costs.

Software subscriptions, overheads, and staff salaries are just some of the regular expenses that bookkeeping practices will need to factor into their pricing. If you fail to do this, you might find that you struggle to break even or even find yourself operating at a loss.

- Underestimating pricing: Many bookkeepers are afraid to overcharge or undercharge. Charge too much and potential clients will see you as "too expensive" and go elsewhere, but charge too little and you risk not making a profit.

Am I charging too much, or am I not charging enough? It's a valid question, especially when you are just starting out. The pitfall here though is that bookkeepers often end up underestimating their rates because they are afraid to overcharge their clients.

For example, let's say you offer Xero reconciliation services. You might be regularly working with a small business client who you charge $120 for this service. Another client might enquire about this service, and you might quote them the same price. However, it might turn out that the new client has a lot more transactions to reconcile than your existing client, which means that you end up charging them the same price for a lot more work. Basically, you end up undercharging them. Often, these bookkeepers then end up too scared to tell their clients that they need to charge them more, as they are worried they'll think they are "ripping them off".

My advice would be to always consider the value of your time and think about quoting on the job based on the volume of work and complexity rather than giving the client a fixed one-size-fits-all price upfront. Also, if you do decide to go the hourly rate route, always make sure you are quoting appropriately. Don't assume that a particular task will take the same amount of time for one client as it did for another, as more often than not, this will result in you undercharging. Always be sure to clarify the scope of the work (in this case, the volume of transactions), and make sure you are quoting a price that is appropriate for the amount of time and effort that will be involved in completing the task.

Don't be too conservative – it's always better to err on the side of caution, and charge slightly more if you are unsure than it is to end up significantly undercharging.

- Selling yourself short: Another common mistake made by new bookkeeping businesses is that they will take on new clients and new business at a low price just to start getting clients in the door. Although this may be what you need to do to start with, a lot of bookkeepers then fall into trap of keeping up this mindset, and being too willing to negotiate down on the price any time a client pushes back against it – even if they know the price they are quoting is reflective of their expertise and the time and effort it will take them to complete the work.

An example could be if you quoted someone $250 a month for your services. They might tell you that is too expensive, and ask if you can do it for $120 a month instead because they obtained another cheaper quote from a different bookkeeper. Many bookkeepers will agree, because they want to compete on price and don't want a potential client to go with a competitor, even if that means they end up under-pricing their services. However, this often means they end up operating at a loss. If your prices are too cheap, not only are you not charging what you're worth but you're also probably not charging enough to cover your costs and allow for a profit margin on top of that. The other thing to remember is that the other bookkeepers may not include exactly the same things you do in the same service. I have seen many cases where I have taken over a file for reconciliation work and found there are no attached invoices, and so on.

For your bookkeeping business to be a success, you need to stop selling yourself short and focus on attracting clients to your business that fit – that is, those who see the value in the services you are offering and who are prepared to pay you what you are worth. You are not here to be "cheap" or "affordable" – you are here to offer high-quality bookkeeping services that add real value for your clients. If a potential client is pushing back on your prices and pressuring you to cut them in half, they are not the type of client you want to work with.

- Not knowing your value: So often, bookkeepers feel like they have to compete to offer the "cheapest" or "most affordable" bookkeeping services in order to be able to compete with their competitors. However, there is another way that you can be competitive, whilst still demanding the rates that you deserve – and that is to know and be able to articulate your value.

To find your value, you need to look at your services through the eyes of your client and think: *What do they perceive as being of value?* You could also look at this through a different lens and think: *What problem are you going to be solving for them?* From there, you can then move on to, *what is it worth to my clients to be able to solve that problem,* in other words, *what will they pay me to solve that problem for them?*

Many bookkeepers think that the value they provide to their clients is their bookkeeping services. Wrong! Any bookkeeper can provide these services to their clients, but your value is what you can specifically bring to the table, or why clients should choose you and pay more for you.

For some bookkeepers, their value might be that they can offer the cheapest price, and sure, this might be what some clients see as valuable. However, this doesn't align with your vision to run a successful and profitable bookkeeping business where you are paid what you are worth. Instead, think of your value as how much time you can save your clients; how much easier you can make things for them; how much stress and headaches you can save them; how you can give them peace of mind; and how much more convenient you can make their day-to-day lives.

## Know your worth, and choose clients who are prepared to pay you accordingly

If there is one piece of advice I can give you, it's to know your value. Choose clients who know your worth and who are prepared to pay accordingly.

Generally speaking, the best kinds of clients will be those who recognise the value that you are able to offer to them, as they will be more likely to accept the rates that you send and rarely question bills and timesheets and so on. By comparison, clients who are more cost focused can be more painful to work with, as they are often on the lookout for ways to cut costs as much as possible, and may question the rates you are charging them as being "too expensive" despite the expertise and value you are providing them with.

For this reason, once you hit the $250k mark and can afford to focus more on the target client profiles for whom you really want to be working, my suggestion would be to focus more on pursuing clients who see the value that you bring to them, rather than those who are only focusing on cost. You will also be able to start letting go of clients who are neither profitable, nor a fit for your business, or who are too focused on price rather than the value you create for them.

# Chapter 6: Achieving Balance and Adjusting Pricing

In the last chapter, we explored the importance of setting prices that reflect what you're worth, along with the expertise and value you are delivering to your clients. As mentioned though, as your business grows, the time will come when it is time to put your prices up. In this chapter, we will be building on what we discussed in the last chapter by focusing on how to manage price increases in your bookkeeping practice.

There will come a time in your business journey when you are enjoying enough growth and stability that you are in a position to think about putting your prices up so that they better reflect your expertise and the value you are delivering to your clients. As a general rule of thumb, this will happen at around the $150-500k mark, which will usually be the point at which you will start to think about refining your pricing and your product to maximise your revenue. You will also be able to afford to be choosier about the types of clients you take on, and will have the luxury of being able to work with only your ideal clients whose values and vision align with your own. That being said, though, this may happen for you sooner or later, depending on the types of products and services that you offer, the types of clients that you are targeting, and your goals for growing your business.

Essentially, you will reach this stage when you find your hours are maxed out, and you have a choice to make: bring on more clients and work harder, or work smarter for more. The first instinct of many bookkeeping businesses will be to take on more clients and more work. The reality is though that if your goal is to maximise your profits whilst enjoying financial freedom and a better work–life balance, you need to be working smarter, not harder. This means raising your prices, so that you are working with higher-paying clients who can add real value to your business. You'll be doing the same things, but you'll be earning more for doing them.

## Signs that it's time to raise your prices

When it's time to raise your prices, you'll know because you'll be feeling like you're capped or restricted by what you're currently charging, as well as seeing it in your financial metrics. If running a successful bookkeeping practice or company is your goal, then maximising your growth and profitability is key, so it's important that you are able to recognise when the right time is to raise your prices and get paid what you are really worth.

Here are a few of the key signs that it's the right time for you to raise your prices:

- You are experiencing more and more demand and taking on more and more work, and are finding that your hours are consistently getting maxed out or you are getting booked out weeks in advance. All of these are signs that your bookkeeping business is experiencing more demand than it is able to keep up with.

  Whilst some businesses might say that there is no such thing as "too much demand", I would beg to differ. If you work too hard, you risk getting burnt out, and you are likely to start feeling stressed or your mental health may begin to suffer. When your business gets to this point, you have two choices: grow your team to keep up with the increased demand, or raise your prices.

By raising your prices, you can exit the lower-paying clients and reduce your workload whilst generating the same or a greater amount of profit.

- You have the lowest prices in the market. If you do competitor research and find that you are offering the lowest prices in the market (for example, you are charging $40 for a particular service and all the other bookkeeping companies in your area are charging $100+), this is not necessarily a good thing.

  Whilst charging lower prices can help you to attract new clients and new business when you are just starting out, this usually backfires because you'll only end up attracting clients who are on the lookout for the cheapest price. This does not align with your vision for creating wealth and maximising your profitability by working with high-value clients. Clients who are looking for maximum value and quality service will not be scrambling to find the lowest price. Instead, they'll be looking for a bookkeeping business that offers the best standard of service, and will be prepared to pay more for this if necessary, so it is these clients that you need to be targeting – not those who are looking for the cheapest price.

- If your prices have been the same for a long time, this is another sign that it's time for you to raise them. With current rates of inflation and the rising cost of living, most businesses incrementally increase their prices in order to be able to keep up, and your business should be no exception.

For example, if you've been operating since 2015 and haven't updated your pricing since then, it's definitely time to update your prices.

- If you're not covering your costs, this is another indicator that it's time to put your prices up. This kind of ties into the previous point – with inflation and the rising cost of living, the price of almost everything has been going up, and your recurring expenses and overheads will be no exception.

As a bookkeeping business, you will have various expenses that you have to pay – which will vary from office premises, electricity, and internet to things like staff wages and software subscriptions. It is highly likely that the cost of these things has been creeping up over the past few years, which means that if you haven't been incrementally raising your prices accordingly, you may be operating at a loss or with a much smaller profit margin once all of your expenses are deducted.

If you're finding that you're not covering all of your costs or are not making as much profit on your services as you used to, it's time to raise your pricing.

- If you feel overworked and underpaid, this is another sign to raise your prices. Maybe you really dislike completing certain tasks for your clients and think you should be getting paid more for them, or maybe you're just feeling like the amount you're charging doesn't reflect the time and effort that you're putting in for your clients.

As a business owner, you need to be making sure that the prices you are setting are worth your time. Rather than worrying about what your customers might think, you need to focus on what's best for you and your business – and that means setting prices that accurately reflect your time, effort, and the value you are creating for your clients.

## Approaches for increasing your pricing

Once you've decided to increase your prices, there are a few different ways you can go about doing this. For example, you can:

- Raise your fixed price services (for example, by increasing the price of your fixed price packages by 10%).

- Raise your hourly rate (for example, rather than $50 an hour, charging $60 an hour).

- Making small changes and incrementally raising your fees over time (for example, increasing your rates by $10 every year, or financial year). This means you are putting your prices up over a couple of years, rather than increasing them significantly in one go.

- Reducing your inclusions but keeping the price the same (for example, if you offer 20 hours of your time for a $1,000 monthly retainer, shrinking the size of the offer so that only 15 hours are included).

- Better articulating your service offering so that you are more clearly communicating what you are offering and how you can add value for your clients.

- Stopping the "freebies" (for example, if you offer physical products and cover the shipping fee, you could pass this charge on to your clients instead, rather than absorbing the cost. You could do the same if you offer subscriptions of accounting software or expense payable software and previously have bundled this in – perhaps you start charging for it).

The best strategy for increasing prices will vary from business to business based on a range of factors, including the services and products you offer, your goals as a business, the types of clients you offer, and your current size and revenue. You could decide to use only one of these price increase strategies or a combination to increase your pricing across your business.

Whatever approach you decide to take, by increasing your prices, you are taking the first steps on your journey to creating more wealth and achieving more freedom within your business.

**How to communicate price changes to your clients**

Once you have made the decision to raise your prices, there are a few key things that you will need to do and keep in mind when communicating these changes to your clients. For example, you will need to:

1. Provide your clients with sufficient warning. Nobody likes to be surprised, so don't tell your clients that your prices have gone up a couple of days before their next

invoice is due. Ideally, you should aim to alert your clients of your price changes two or three months in advance. At the very least, you should give them a month's notice.

By alerting your clients well in advance, you are providing them with ample opportunity to understand the changes and how these will affect them. You are also giving them enough time to ask questions and seek clarification where necessary to ensure they are completely clear about the new pricing.

2. Send your clients an email notifying them of the price increase in writing. This should be clear and easy to understand, and tell them everything they need to know about the price changes and how this impacts them. In this letter, you should:

- Thank your clients and express your appreciation to them. Rather than jumping straight in with the details of the price increase, open with a line or two thanking them for their support and for choosing your business. This makes them feel valued, which means they will be more likely to stick with you despite your price increase.

   For example: *"Hi (name). Thank you again for choosing (business name) for all of your bookkeeping needs. Your support means so much to us, and we are excited to continue looking after your books for you in future."*

- Be clear about the price increase and the time at which this will come into effect. You need to make sure that your clients are completely clear about the price changes, including how much your prices are increasing by and when the increase will come into effect.

Be confident when you communicate to your clients that you have increased your prices - don't feel that this is something you need to apologise for. It is fine if you want to provide some explanation for why the price increase was necessary, but don't start going into too much detail or making excuses for it.

Also, be sure to effectively communicate the value of your higher rates - for example, that increasing your prices will allow you to continue to offer them the best quality standard of service.

For example, "*At (business name), we are committed to offering you the very best quality bookkeeping services. Although we have tried our best to keep our pricing the same, our operational costs have increased significantly over the past year, which means we have made the difficult decision to increase our prices by (amount). This will allow us to ensure that we are still able to offer you the best possible standard of service.*

*These changes will come into effect on (date). Until then, you will still be charged at the old rate of (amount).*"

Remember, the types of clients you are targeting are those who recognise your value and are prepared to invest more in your services and pay you what you're worth. So, by communicating with them about the value of your higher rates, you are providing them with confidence that you can continue to provide them with maximum value.

- Try and find a way to add extra value if you can – for example, by articulating the value you are creating or moving them into another level of service at a discounted price. By doing this, clients may be less hesitant to accept the change in price as they will feel that they are getting something for free, which outweighs the perceived increased cost of the change.

- Invite them to ask questions if there's anything they are unsure of or wish to clarify about the price increase. For example, "*If you have any questions or concerns, please feel free to reach out. I would be more than happy to answer any questions that you have about this price increase.*"

- Add a warm closing like "*Thank you again for being such a great client*".

3. After sending out your price increase email, send your clients a reminder. For example, if you sent out your price increase letter or email three months in advance, the month before the price changes are due to come into effect, send them another email to remind them of the changes.

4. Update your contracts. Once your clients have agreed to the increased prices, you will then need to update your contracts or agreements that you have with that client to reflect the price change.

This will ensure that you have a formal record of them agreeing to the increased prices, which will offer you protection in future should any of your clients turn around and claim they were unaware of the price changes.

5. Be sure to plan for future price increases. Your pricing strategy should be a part of your overarching business strategy, and should be something that you are continuously reassessing and re-evaluating as necessary to ensure that you continue to charge accordingly for the level of expertise, quality of service, and value you provide to your clients.

For example, you might decide that you'll be increasing your prices by 10% each financial year, in which case you'll need to plan ahead and start this process over again each financial year, to ensure your clients are adequately informed about the price increases that will take place in the year ahead. Likewise, you might make a plan to do some competitor research at the end of each financial year to ensure you are still pricing your services accordingly, and then make any adjustments required to your pricing strategy.

## Losing clients when you raise your prices

Any time you raise your prices, there is always the chance that you might end up losing some of your clients – particularly those who are more cost focused, and who are looking for the lowest price or cheapest deal.

You'll know who these clients are, because they'll be the ones who say "Bookkeeper X is offering this service for half the price. Can you match it?" or "That's not in my budget. Can you do it for $x instead?" These clients will always be trying to haggle you down on price, which may not align with your vision or ideal client.

These clients are not the ideal clients that you want to be working for, so if they do push back on your pricing, don't be afraid to release them. See this as opening up more room for clients who know your worth, and who are prepared to pay you accordingly for the value you can create for them.

Remember that the loss of money from clients who leave will be offset by the increased rate at which you will be charging those who continue using your services.

# Chapter 7: Overcoming the Fear of Raising Prices

Like many business owners, you might find that you have some deep-rooted fears around raising your prices that are holding you back from unlocking your bookkeeping business's full potential.

I experienced the same fears in the early days of running my own business. I noticed that I would price a service up and then I would reduce it, as I thought it was too much and the client would not pay. What I found is those that haggled on price, frequently turned out to be rather painful and expected so much, and I would often repeatedly make a loss on the client month after month. Those same clients would not respect scope of work outlines and get you to do more and more, yet not want to pay for the additional services. A number of conversations would happen in regard to the necessity to move up packages or scale back the client's requests, and most of the time this simply did not happen – the work would just keep coming, and then some more.

Even though the conversations were difficult, I needed to remind myself I was not responsible for their business, only for mine, and that our work is valuable and we deserved to get paid. This was extremely difficult at times as the people were lovely and I wanted to do the right thing by them, especially when they were experiencing hard business times.

When you move these clients out, you will find it opens the space for new clients to step into. These clients will be a better fit, as you will have learnt so much about yourself and your business that you are now able to articulate what you expect and the value you will deliver.

Let's take a look at some of the common fears around price increases, and how you can overcome these to transform the profitability of your business and help you achieve your "why".

1. "I'll lose my clients if I put my prices up": This is a very common fear held by many bookkeepers who worry that they will lose their existing clientele if they put their prices up. As we discussed previously though, the clients you lose when you put your prices up are going to be those who put price first – that is, they are looking for the cheapest service or lowest price out there. These kinds of clients do not align with your "why", which is to generate wealth and create a profit for your business, so it doesn't matter if you lose them, because they're not adding value for you and your business.

   On the other hand, the types of clients who do add value for you and your business are unlikely to be put off by a price increase, because they see your worth and are prepared to pay you appropriately for your skills, expertise, and the value you create for them and their business. These are the clients you want to be attracting and retaining, so if you lose some lower-value clients along the way, don't worry – you're simply creating more room for these higher-value clients who are a better fit for your business.

2. "Clients won't come to me if my prices are too high": This is another common misconception that ties in with the previous one. Again, there are some clients out there for whom price will be their main concern. However, these are not the types of clients that you want to be servicing.

   Your target clients are those who are prepared to invest in high-quality bookkeeping services that create value for them and their business, and who are prepared to pay you what you are worth. Sure, your higher prices might not attract those price-focused clients who are always looking for the cheapest price or best deal. However, by setting your prices higher, you'll be weeding out these low-value prospects to ensure you are only attracting clients who are prepared to invest in their businesses through quality bookkeeping services that add real value.

3. "My clients won't want to pay more for my services": This is a big assumption, because how do you know that your clients won't want to pay more for your services unless you ask them? Chances are anyway that if you're working with clients who are able to see the value you create for them, rather than just a number of hours or a dollar figure, they will be more than happy to stick with you and honour the new price.

   You can also help your clients to see why it is worth investing more in the value you create for them by effectively communicating this in the price increase email or letter you send them. You can use this letter to explain to your clients how this price increase will allow you to continue to provide them with value. By helping your clients to clearly see why the price increase is justified and how it will help you to help them better, they are likely to be happy to pay more.

4. "I don't know what to say": The conversation about price increases can be a difficult one to have, especially if you have never raised your prices before. The good news is that with practice, it becomes a lot easier, and by the time you've adjusted your pricing a few times, you'll be a pro at communicating these changes to your clients.

5. "Why would my clients pay more for my services?": This fear is a classic example of imposter syndrome at its finest, and if you're thinking like this, you're certainly not alone. Many bookkeepers (and other business owners for that matter) find themselves questioning why clients would pay more for their services, particularly if they can get the same kind of service elsewhere for much less.

Remember, your clients are paying you for the value that *you* deliver. This value that you deliver is what makes you unique, and is what makes you stand out from all the other bookkeeping businesses out there. Your clients are paying you because you create value for their business, and are the one who can help them to solve whatever problem they have at present. From their point of view, the solution or outcome that you will help them to achieve is worth the greater investment in your services.

All of these common fears can hold you back from raising your prices, but it's not until you step outside your comfort zone that you will be able to remove the barriers that have been limiting the growth of your business, and, until now, your profits.

My advice would be to take a long, hard look at the current thoughts, beliefs, and misconceptions you have around pricing. The more you think about these things, the more that you will still start to notice some of the fears and limiting beliefs that have been holding you back. Once you are able to recognise these, you will then be able to start doing the work to face your fears and overcome them.

Remember, fear is a natural response any time we do something that is unfamiliar to us or that we are unsure about. However, it's also something that we can get comfortable with, because growing your business means stepping out into the unknown sometimes and facing your fears head on.

So, know your "why" and let this guide you in the right direction, even if that means having to first overcome your fears. In the long term, your courage will pay off in a big way for you and your business when you are finally getting paid what you are worth!

# Section 3: Scaling and Workflow

# Chapter 8: Do What You Love (and Delegate, Automate, or Eliminate the Rest!)

**Doing it all**

When starting any kind of business, the main objective (for the first year or so at least) will be to drive as much new business to you as possible. That means connecting with new clients and taking on as much work from them as you can to generate the maximum amount of revenue possible to your business. This will play an important role in ensuring your business's survival, as well as your ability to eventually pay yourself a wage.

A lot of the time, this will mean that for the first few years of running your own bookkeeping business, you will be wearing all the hats: practice owner, practice manager, business development manager, salesperson, marketing manager, operations manager, bookkeeper, and so on.

You will also usually end up taking on anything and everything to begin with. Even though your goal may be to become more specialised and only offer a handful of services, you might find that you need to be more general to start with, to drive as much revenue and attract as many new customers to your business as possible in order to survive.

Until then though, it's important to strike the right balance between not taking on enough and taking on too much. Take on too little, and you won't be attracting enough new customers and driving enough revenue into your business to keep it afloat. But take on too much, and you'll end up stressed, burnt out, and stuck.

In the first couple of years of running your business, there will be a lot to get done and you'll be doing it alone for the most part. The biggest piece of advice I can give you is to be strategic and prioritise everything you need to get done, and focus on completing one task at a time. When you focus on too many things at once, your progress will be very slow, so do one thing through to completion then start on the next thing.

**Automation, delegation, or elimination**

When you hit around the $250–500k mark, you can focus on becoming more specialised so that you're focusing on only a few key areas. This will allow you to spend more time focusing on tasks that interest you and that you are passionate about, as well as those that demand your personal attention, skill set, and expertise.

At this stage, you will also be able to afford to be more choosy when it comes to the types of clients and projects that you take on. You will be in the position to take on only clients and projects that are a good fit for you and your business and which align with your business goals and personal values, and decline those that are not a great fit.

When you reach this point, you have three choices to deal with tasks and activities that do not interest you, or which do not need to be completed by you personally. These are:

- Automate: Whereas once we would have had to complete certain repetitive and time-consuming tasks manually, recent advances in technology mean that we can now use artificial intelligence (AI) to automate these, so that we can spend more time focusing on tasks that require our manual input or personal expertise and skill set. For example, many modern bookkeeping software programs, like Xero and MYOB, allow you to automatically import financial data in from other sources, meaning you no longer have to spend time manually copying this information over from one platform to another.

- Delegate: This is where you either hire another staff member (if money permits) or outsource to a subcontractor, who will then be responsible for completing tasks that either you do not want to do or you don't have the time to complete personally. For example, you might hire an assistant for five hours per week who is responsible for doing all the admin work, so that you are then able to spend your time focusing on bookkeeping work that requires your expertise and skill set.

- Eliminate: This is where you eliminate (or get rid of) certain activities that are not benefitting you or your business, or which do not align with your vision, goals, and pathway to achieving your "why". For example, in the earlier years of your business, you might find yourself completing many smaller ad hoc jobs for various small businesses and clients who do not pay much. If creating wealth and making money is your goal, you might decide to get rid of these smaller bookkeeping jobs and low-paying clients, and instead focus on working with larger clients on a higher-paying retainer basis.

I started out by employing someone that allowed me to work on higher-level tasks. This was a game changer for me. As an example of how this impacts the bottom line: I have 30 hours available for me to work per week, however, I spend ten of those on admin tasks. If I switch this to five additional hours a week and outsource five hours at $40 per hour, then I have created an extra $275 in my business per week working the same number of hours. This equates to an extra $14,300 per year. The more you can delegate and focus on multiplier events, the more your income will thank you for it.

By automating, delegating, or eliminating these other activities, you will be able to spend more time concentrating on the parts of your business that are of the most interest and value to you. This will give you more focus when working towards your business goals, as well as enhance your personal satisfaction with your business journey.

# Chapter 9: Work Like a Snowball

Working out where you are headed also means setting yourself goals or targets that you would like to achieve at different stages of your business journey. You might set these goals or targets based on a certain amount of revenue that you expect to generate (e.g. what do you want to achieve when you are earning $50k, $100k, $250k, and beyond?) or a certain number of clients you expect to attract (e.g. what are some of the things you would like to achieve when you have five, ten, thirty, or fifty customers, and so on?)

The specific hurdles that you set yourself at each stage will depend on the specific goals that you have, and what your priorities are when it comes to what you hope to get out of running your own bookkeeping practice. As a general rule of thumb though, here are some of the hurdles you can expect to overcome as you grow your business and attain different levels of revenue:

- $100k – At this level of revenue, you will be taking on everything yourself. The money you make will be used to ensure the survival of your business, as well as to pay yourself a wage. Start delegating some tasks where possible via a subcontractor, casual, or part-time arrangement.

- $200k – At this level of revenue, you will likely be investing more in marketing to drive more leads to your business.

You will also be creating simple systems and standard operating procedures to help your business become more efficient so that you can take on more work and get it done more quickly and efficiently.

- $250k – When you hit this mark, you might want to think about growing your team and subcontracting or hiring someone part- or full-time to help you. This stage of growth is likely to be all about the HR side of things, which means finding people that fit and the best ways for them to support you and your business.

  You should also start focusing on setting up systems to scale beyond $500k, and invest time in defining your ideal client type and understanding this in more detail. It's at this point that you can start being choosy and really start honing in on who your ideal clients to work with would be.

- $500k – At this level of revenue, it's all about scaling. That means refining your pricing and your product to maximise your revenue, and ensuring your processes are running as smoothly and efficiently as possible.

  You will also want to take a more strategic approach to marketing to ensure you are targeting your ideal customers in the best possible way.

  You may also want to think about creating a management team, with key personnel who can take over running your business from a day-to-day and high-level management point of view. This is another task you can delegate to these key personnel, which is one less thing that you need to do personally.

- $500–750k – As you work your way up from $500k to $750k, your focus should be on managing relationships with key clients and referral partners. Get strategic about these relationships, and think about how you can get maximum benefit from them whilst providing the other person with maximum benefit as well – it should go both ways!

- $750k+ – Once you've hit the $750k+ mark, now is the time for you to exit the business and let it run itself. By now, you will have engaged all the key personnel you need to support the smooth day-to-day running of your business, so it is the perfect time for you to start taking more of a hands-off role if that is what you desire. You can still keep a hand in the business and "check and correct", meaning you set the overall targets and expectations for the business and manage your people as they work towards this. However, there will be less need for you to be working full-time on the day-to-day running of your business unless you choose to.

I like to think of this approach as "working like a snowball", because you are growing your business year on year and building an asset. Your revenue will be derived from the same types of products and services and the same repetitive tasks. However, as you take on more clients, make more sales, and continue to refine and improve your processes so you can do everything quicker and better, your revenue will continue to grow and grow – just like a snowball.

# Chapter 10: Building the Right Team

When you've reached the point in your business where you are ready to start delegating certain tasks to somebody else, the next step will be to start thinking about how to surround yourself with the right team.

Generally speaking, this will usually happen at around the $100–250k mark. However, you may find that you reach the point of needing to hire someone sooner or later than this. When you are "ready" will depend on a range of factors, including the types of services you offer, the volume of work that you take on, and the amount you charge for your services.

### What kind of staff do I need?

When it comes to the types of staff that you need to hire for your bookkeeping practice, again this is something that will be largely determined by the kinds of services that you offer, as well as the types of tasks that you will be looking to outsource.

Generally speaking, it may be more affordable to take on your additional team members as a freelancer or independent contractor for a few hours a week to start with. Over time, as your business grows, you can always start looking at growing their employment to part- or even full-time, when your workload and the value that person brings to your business justifies this.

Administrative, marketing, and bookkeeping assistants, receptionists, practice managers, and even a second or third bookkeeper, are all examples of additional staff who you may wish to take on in your bookkeeping business. You might even wish to diversify your service offering by taking on team members like accountants, business analysts, or other professionals who offer complementary services to those that you provide.

As your business grows, you will gain more insight into the areas where you feel you require additional support, or where you would like to delegate certain tasks. You can then focus on finding the right team members in the right roles to support your business over time.

Remember, the idea is to take on staff who can help take some of the pressure off you by attending to tasks that do not require your personal skill set, expertise, or attention. That way, you will have more time to spend concentrating on higher-level tasks or those that will make you the most money.

You will recall that the example we used earlier was hiring an assistant as a freelancer or independent contractor for a few hours a week. That person could then take care of all the admin work for you, so that you can then spend your time focusing on bookkeeping work that requires your expertise and skill set.

## How do I know if I can afford to take on another employee?

The right time to take someone on will be when you hit a time constraint or even before you "think" you can afford to. You need to remember, taking on assistance will increase your income if you are reallocating your hours to multiplier tasks.

A common thought pattern that many business owners fall into, even when they hit around the $100–250k mark (which will usually be when you can afford to start thinking about taking someone else on), is that "I don't have enough money to take someone on". However, making this investment in someone else is actually one of the best ways for you to also invest in the overall success of your business.

Here's how. Remember how, earlier in this book, we talked about how one of the disadvantages of operating as a bookkeeping business can be that you are limited by your own time? Time is a finite resource and we only have so much of it, which means that we are only able to take on so much work within the amount of time that we have available. This can limit your ability to make money.

By outsourcing some of the work that goes into running your business to someone else, you are essentially creating more hours. For instance, if we go back to our previous example where you outsource all of your admin work to an assistant for five hours per week, you are basically opening up five extra hours of time that you wouldn't have had otherwise.

In these five hours, you will be able to take on more higher-level tasks, or tasks that will actually earn your business money. For a bookkeeping practice, this could be carrying out actual bookkeeping tasks rather than admin, which could make you $40, $50, $60, or even more per hour depending on your billing rates or by spending time sourcing leads into the business. Basically, you will be earning more per hour either immediately or in the near future than you would completing all that admin work yourself behind the scenes.

Even if you have to pay $30 an hour to the assistant that you are outsourcing the admin work to, you will still be making a profit on the higher-level work you are carrying out yourself, which therefore makes this a more productive and profitable use of your time in ensuring the financial success of your business. This makes the investment in a new team member worthwhile. In fact, the earlier, the better.

**What makes for a "good" team member?**

Exactly what a "good" team member looks like will very much depend on the type of role that you are looking to fill within your bookkeeping practice. For example, the required skill set and personal attributes for an administrative assistant or receptionist will look very different to those for a marketing assistant!

There are a few different types of staff you may be looking to take on as you grow your bookkeeping practice. Here are a few examples of what skills and attributes you would be looking for, or what makes for a "good" team member in each of these roles (bearing in mind that a team member can be directly hired staff, subcontractors, or outsourced solutions):

- Administrative assistance: For administrative roles, you would be looking for aspects like good time management, organisation, attention to detail, computer skills, and proficiency at completing a range of administrative tasks.

- Receptionists: For a customer-facing role, your new team member will require skills like communication, interpersonal skills, and a commitment to providing exceptional customer service. You will also want someone with good people skills and phone etiquette, who can multi-task, manage competing priorities, and remain calm under pressure.

- Marketing assistance: For marketing roles, you would be looking for skills like creativity, project management, and analytical skills. You would also be looking for technical skills in the types of marketing you are interested in (for example, digital marketing, content writing, or social media).

- Bookkeeper/bookkeeping assistants: For bookkeeping roles, good maths and numeracy skills, a keen eye for detail, accuracy, critical thinking, and problem-solving skills are all skills you would be looking for in your new team member.

Whilst these are some examples of specific skills that you might be looking for in new team members in these roles, there are also some more general ones that will apply to any new staff member that you take on – for example, good communication and teamwork skills. These kinds of skills are important in ensuring the smooth day-to-day running of the business and effective communication amongst your team.

Below are some of the things I would encourage you to actively seek:

- Some people have a genuine interest in your business doing well. Others see it as a job, so look for someone who is as invested in the success of your business as you are.

- You can always train someone on the specifics of a role, however, self-motivation is something to look out for.
- Where your budget allows, always go for the higher skill set. The amount of time you will spend reviewing, training, and redoing work will outweigh the higher skill set cost and it will leave you more at ease.
- Always do reference checks. I have been caught out by this one myself!
- If someone doesn't fit, I promise someone who is a better fit will turn up. Don't try to fit a round peg into a square hole!
- Recruit for someone a step ahead of where you require. This means that, for example, you may need someone to help with data entry. However, you may need them in a number of months to be able to communicate effectively with clients. Always remember where the role is heading to, not the immediate requirement.

When building a team for your bookkeeping business, it is important that you are able to recognise the personal strengths of each of your team members, as well as the unique skills and experiences that they bring to the table. By recognising these things, you will then be able to tap into them and allow each team member to play to their strengths when it comes to how they can best support you and your business.

## Strategies for staff recruitment

There are a few different ways that you might go about recruiting new team members for your bookkeeping practice. The best strategy for staff recruitment for you and your business will depend on a range of factors, including the types of roles you are wanting to fill and how much money you can afford to spend on recruiting the right candidate. Whether or not you have an existing network you can tap into will also play a role in determining the best approach to take to reach the best people for your business.

For one thing, you can always go the traditional route of posting job advertisements on platforms like Seek and Indeed. Alternatively, you might look for staff on networking platforms such as LinkedIn, or solicit word-of-mouth referrals from among your network of contacts. You might also reach out to people you know or with whom you have worked previously, who you think have the right skills and experience to be an asset to your business. When your business is more established, you could even use the services of a professional recruitment firm or offshore recruitment companies who are experienced in recruiting for the kinds of roles that you are looking to fill.

If you are going to be carrying out the recruitment process yourself, you will generally start by identifying suitable candidates for the role – either by soliciting applications through the traditional recruitment process, or by reaching out to people within your network. Once you have identified a few possible candidates who you feel will be well suited for the role, you will usually have an interview with them where you will discuss the role with them further. This will provide you with an opportunity to get to know each other better, so you can see if you "click" and are on the same page professionally. After this, you will usually have a better idea of who the best candidate for the role would be, and you will be able to make an offer of employment to that person.

As we touched on previously, most of the time you will be recruiting your new team members for a few hours a week on a contract basis at first. Over time though, you will be able to look at growing this to part- or full-time employment.

Recruitment in itself is a skill. Getting the right person in the business is extremely valuable, as getting the wrong person can cost thousands of dollars. A few key things to remember:

- Have a job description ready to go and give that to the potential candidate.
- Make sure the potential candidate has the right salary expectation from the onset.
- Listen to the person you are interviewing. Let them speak and ask questions which have a "how did you do" or "what did you do?" This will provide you with some very valuable insights around their character.
- Be prepared for the interview. Use a list of questions and record the answers, and you will be able to start identifying patterns.
- Consider using a personality test to identify what type of skill set they have. This is a great way of seeing personality traits so you can get a more rounded team.
- Make sure you consider getting references. Always ensure one is a professional reference.
- Make sure they do a skills test, especially if they are located offshore. This does not have to be complicated, however, it helps to ensure that their local experience is what you expect it to be.

- Check if the person expects a considerable amount of training outside your organisation. You often see this in highly skilled professionals who have come out of larger practices, as they may expect you to also pay these types of expenses.
- If you see a concern early, call it quickly and remove them from the business. Holding on has a larger impact the longer you don't take corrective action.
- Consider getting a recruitment specialist to set up the questions and take you through the first experience. It will help immensely and you will learn a number of tricks and tips.

**Retaining staff**

When we talk about retention, we are basically talking about how to retain staff within your bookkeeping business. As a business owner, once you find the right people, you understandably want them to stay with your business for as long as possible. There are a few things that you can do to achieve this, to make your business a place where your people love working and where they feel well supported in their careers.

Here are a few of the biggest keys to retention:

- Recognition: When it comes to retention, I would say that one of the biggest things that you can do as a business owner is to ensure that your staff feel appreciated and recognised for the work that they do. Nobody likes feeling like their hard work is going unnoticed, so make sure you call out great work and always recognise your team members for their accomplishments. This will boost morale and ensure that your team members feel motivated and confident about what they do, which in turn makes them more likely to stay with your business.

- Opportunities to use their skills: Business owners often make the mistake of only using their team members for the roles that they are hired to do. However, if your team members have other skills that fall outside the traditional scope of their role, you may as well use them! For example, if you have someone who is currently working as an administrative assistant but who has expressed an interest in more creative tasks, why not incorporate some elements of marketing into their role? By giving your staff the opportunity to do what interests them and what they enjoy, you are again making them more likely to stay with your business.

- Opportunity to grow: This point ties into the previous one, but career progression opportunities (or the opportunity for people to grow beyond their current role) is another thing that plays a big role in the overall retention piece. Look for opportunities to engage your team through professional development and training that will allow them to develop new skills and increase their knowledge to support your business vision. For example, we have upskilled bookkeepers into advice and training roles, administrative assistants into client onboarding roles, and so on.

Also, look for opportunities to recruit up within your company. Rather than taking on an external candidate, could a vacancy be filled by an existing member of your team who is keen to take on more responsibilities or try something within the business? Businesses who do these things are essentially investing in the growth of their team members, which again makes them more engaged and more likely to stay loyal to the business. I would, however, do this with caution, as it is easy to move someone up into the role, but if they don't perform, you need to be able to move them back into the other role. Just make sure they have the ability to be trained, follow process, and most importantly, ask questions when unsure. It may seem logical to ask questions – however, I have noticed that some people won't which presents the risk of the work being done incorrectly.

- Work–life balance: A good work–life balance plays an important role in ensuring the positive mental health and wellbeing of your team. If your team feel overworked and are struggling with long hours and huge workloads, they are more likely to experience burn-out. By comparison, if you focus on becoming more efficient as a company (for example, by streamlining processes, eliminating bottlenecks, and automating where possible), your staff will be able to do more in less time, reducing the chances of them feeling overworked or burnt out. I personally think this one is vital – being a remote bookkeeping business, we are very conscious of team members clocking off as they can tend to keep working. If you notice members working outside standard hours, you need to review processes or hire additional team members.

- Ask them for input: Nobody likes working in a business that is more of a dictatorship than a democracy. Although, as the business owner, you will have the ultimate control over the vision, direction, and day-to-day running of the company, it is highly recommended that you consult with your people and ask them for their thoughts about any issues concerning the business. For example, what do they think works well? What do they think doesn't work so well? What would they like to see changed, or what do they think can be improved within the business? Asking for feedback and involving your team in decision making will ensure that your staff feel heard and validated. It further allows team members to take ownership. This is a critical component – if staff members take ownership of the process/role, then you will notice increased care in regard to the business. It will also allow you to gain valuable insights into possible issues that may be causing staff dissatisfaction, which you can then act on to promote retention within the business.

o A simple thing to implement in the business is what I call a check and correct. I emphasise that you need to communicate that all errors are just learnings and a chance for us to fix the process. It is a simple exercise you use by yourself or with the team. Ask each team member the first two points, then as a team, discover the new process together.

- What did you think worked well this month?
- What did you think didn't work well?
- What should we do again next month?
- What should we do differently next month?

- Giving them the tools they need to succeed: As a business owner, it is your responsibility to give your team members the tools and resources they need to be able to succeed in their roles. Whilst in an ideal world we would all like our new staff to hit the ground running and be working at full capability from day one, the reality is that new staff will usually require some support to get started in their role. By setting up clear policies, procedures, templates, and standard operating procedures for your business, you will be providing your team with a solid foundation to succeed. In reality, I don't think that you need all your systems documented, however, you should definitely aspire to have this completed. What I have personally found super valuable is 15-minute touch points where staff can book time in the diary to go through questions they have. The trick is to allow time as quickly as possible – ideally within a couple of hours of the request. I also get staff to update any process manuals with changes, and at times get them to document a new process.

You should also check in with them regularly during their first few weeks with your business, as this will ensure they feel confident and well supported throughout their transition into their new role. This is vital. I personally have a daily check-in for the first few weeks, then weekly, and then bi-monthly. This really helps team members feel they have access to guidance.

Much of the time, it can be easier to retain staff than it is to attract staff, so when you find the right people, you want to be doing all you can to keep them. For this reason, it is definitely worthwhile investing in the time necessary to ensure your staff are feeling satisfied and supported in their roles. By doing these things, you will be able to maximise the chances of people staying with your company, rather than making the move to a competitor or seeking employment elsewhere. However, the flip side of this is that I strongly believe that people will exit and you should allow them to lovingly. Also, at times, you may need to move them out of the business. Staff turnover does cost the business money, however, you should also welcome new staff into the business. I think hanging on to old staff members who are no longer a fit for the business can have a wider detrimental impact on it.

## When to part ways

As a business owner, it is important to understand that your team needs to consist of the right people with the right skills, who can best support you and the overall success of your business. However, not all of the team members that you take on will be the right fit for you and your business, and it is inevitable that at some point you will need to part ways with a member of your team.

It is important to know that this is not necessarily a reflection of you or the other person, and that very often nobody has done anything wrong. Sometimes people just end up being not the right fit for your business – whether they don't fit your vision or vibration, or you just aren't on the same wavelength any more.

In these cases, the best thing you can do is to release that person lovingly onto their new path, and encourage them as they explore all the new opportunities that are out there waiting for them. And remember, the right person for your business will come along!

## The role of coaches and mentors

Coaches and mentors may not technically be employees, per se, however, they are definitely worth investing in once your bookkeeping practice hits the $200k mark and you are ready to start thinking more strategically about how to grow your business, and thus I would encourage you to get one sooner rather than later.

As a business owner, there are two different types of coaches and mentors with whom you might choose to work on your business journey. The first type is functional/practical, which means coaches and mentors who work with you to help you to overcome challenges and develop the technical skills you need to make your business a success. The second type is mindset, meaning coaches and mentors who can guide you in the developing the kind of mindset you need to succeed as a business owner.

I currently work with people for both. Over the years, I have had several mindset coaches and one of the key takeaways has been that I am responsible for what I create and how I create it, and that I can change it at any time. Every time you reach a mental barrier, they actively work with you to overcome your limiting thought patterns so you can go beyond what you thought was possible.

Functional coaches are also vital. These coaches are people who have taken the journey before you, and they have strategies and know what is coming down the path for you next. It allows you to plan early for the next step and minimises the hit-and-miss approach to getting a result.

When choosing a coach, I would recommend looking for someone who specialises in working with your type of business. A specialised coach with experience in working with business owners to grow successful bookkeeping practices will be able to offer you the most value, as opposed to one who deals with startups or businesses more generally.

Likewise, when it comes to finding a mentor, my advice would be to look for someone who has achieved what you want to achieve, or who has reached the stage of their business that you want to get to. For example, if your ultimate goal is to move from a bookkeeping practice to a successful seven-figure bookkeeping company, look for a mentor who has done this. Likewise, if you are wanting to branch out from just offering bookkeeping services to offering a more comprehensive range of business advisory services, look for a mentor who has done this. The mentor that you choose should be someone who has already walked the path before you, as this way they will be able to provide you with tried and tested recommendations that work to help you achieve your business goals.

# Chapter 11: Managing Difficult Conversations

In the course of running your bookkeeping business, there will be times when you have to have tough discussions with staff and clients. Examples could be if you have to let an employee go because they are no longer a fit for your business, or if you outgrow a client and need to let them go too.

Although these discussions are by no means pleasant to have, they are often necessary in order to move your business forward and bring you closer to achieving your "why". I also like to look at these conversations as often being in the best interests of both parties involved (you and them), as they give both of you the chance to move on to another opportunity that is better aligned with you.

In this chapter, I will be sharing with you some tips for how to effectively manage these difficult conversations with your staff and clients. I will also be giving you some ideas for things you could say to help you feel more confident in managing these tricky situations.

## Subcontractors, outsourced suppliers, and staff

In the course of running your own bookkeeping business, there will be occasions when you have to let one of your team members go. Maybe they are underperforming, or maybe they just don't fit your vision or are no longer on the same wavelength as you.

Whatever the reason, it's important that as a business owner, you understand the need to surround yourself with the right people with the right skills, who can best support you and the overall success of your business. This means that when one of your team members is no longer the right fit for you and your business, you need to know it's time for you to part ways with them.

If you're wondering if it's time to let a team member go, here are some of the indicators that it may be time:

- You do not share the same vision
- You are no longer on the same wavelength
- They are not living by the company's vision
- They are not meeting your performance expectations
- They refuse to take accountability or ownership
- They are reluctant to change, grow, or learn
- They are a poor cultural fit
- They do not have the right mentality
- Their behaviour has changed
- They are having a negative impact on the rest of the team
- They have a negative mindset
- They keep making the same mistakes
- Their expectations regarding salary cannot be supported by the business.

Initially, you should always give the person a chance to improve – for example, by letting them know how they are underperforming, and giving them some examples of how they might be able to improve. You should then give them an opportunity to show that they are trying to improve. If after a time though, their performance or behaviour at work are still not up to scratch, it is likely to be time for the two of you to go your separate ways.

This can be a tough call to have to make, but as a business owner you need to be acting in the best interests of your business. In these situations, the best thing you can do is to release that person onto their new path, and encourage them as they explore all the new opportunities that are out there waiting for them. It is almost certain that there will be a new role out there for which they will be a better fit, and also someone out there who is a better fit for your business. By letting the staff member go who is not the best fit for your business, you are doing both of you a favour.

Still, letting someone go can be a daunting and overwhelming prospect for many business owners, as you feel bad and don't want to upset the team member. To handle this difficult conversation in the best possible way, speak to your employee in person, and try to frame the situation as positively as possible. You might say to your employee:

*"I really appreciate the effort you've been putting in. However, I have noticed that you seem to be distracted/not enjoying the role anymore."*

Listen to what your team member has to say, and come up with a strategy. Perhaps you could even provide them with time to interview elsewhere to support them in finding their new role.

It is important to know that letting an employee go does not mean you have to be rude or disrespectful. Instead, you need to be direct but polite by pointing out the issues that the employee needs to fix, or the reasons why they are not a good fit for your business any more. Keep things non-personal, and try and focus on the positives so that the two of you can part ways on good terms.

## Clients

Just as it will sometimes be time to part ways with a member of your team, there will also come a time when you have to terminate your relationship with a client. Most of the time, these conversations will come about around the $250–500k mark, which is the point at which you can start being pickier about the types of clients that you take on so that you are only working with your "ideal" clients.

Your client might be pushing back on your price increases, not pay on time, or they might be looking for a particular service that you no longer want to offer. They might not fit your values and vision, or they might just be unreasonable or challenging for you to deal with. Maybe you just dread dealing with them. All of these are signs that it may be time for you to terminate your relationship with them.

As you grow as a business, you will outgrow clients and clients will outgrow you and that is alright. Just as with your staff, suppliers, and subcontractors, release them without animosity so they can find someone else who is a better fit for them and what they are looking for.

You might choose to meet with them in person to let them know that you will no longer be working for them, or you might send them an email. Whatever approach you decide to take, the key is to keep it non-personal.

Just as with letting a member of your team go, though, this can be a challenging conversation to have with your clients. Here are some ideas for what you might say:

*"It's been lovely working with you and your team. Unfortunately, I will no longer be able to offer x services. I apologise for the inconvenience, and would be happy to refer you to another bookkeeping practice who are better able to meet your needs."*

*"It's been lovely working with you and your team. Unfortunately, I no longer feel that I am the best fit for your needs, so I am no longer going to be able to offer my services to you from x. I apologise for the inconvenience."*

*"Thank you for working with us for the last x years. Given a change in business strategy, we will not be able to offer you ongoing services. Our services will cease on x."*

As a business owner, it is important that you grow your confidence in having these difficult conversations as they are an unpleasant, albeit necessary, part of your role. With practice, you will become more confident at having these conversations so that you can handle them more effectively in future.

# Chapter 12: Investing in Systems and Processes

Having proper systems and processes in place is key if you want to be able to grow and scale your bookkeeping practice. Generally speaking, systems and processes will be something that you will need to start thinking about once you get to the $200–250k hurdle. In my view, though, there is no harm in investing in key systems and processes earlier, if you have the time and budget to be able to do so. This will provide your business with a solid foundation for growth and expansion, which will only help you when you intend to scale up later on.

## What are systems and processes?

A lot of the time, people use the words "systems" and "processes" interchangeably. Although they are similar and important for the same kinds of reasons, there is a difference between the two.

### Processes

First of all, let's look at processes. A process is basically a series of steps that need to be undertaken in order to perform a particular task. Processes will usually be documented, and will guide you and your team members through how to perform a certain task in a specific way to ensure a particular outcome is achieved.

For example, in a bookkeeping context, you might have processes in place for things such as how to respond to customer enquiries or how to answer the phone. You might also have processes in place around how certain financial reports should be prepared, how invoices should be processed, and how payroll should be carried out.

These are all examples of general processes that most bookkeeping practices have in place, though you may sometimes find that you have other, more specific processes in place too, depending on the types of business activities you carry out. For example, if your marketing strategy is big on thought leadership and content marketing, you might have processes around how a blog post or article for your website should be created. Likewise, if your business model revolves around selling products and services under a company structure (for example, eBooks or templates), you might have processes around how orders should be processed and how these resources should be created.

*Systems*

Now, let's look at systems. Systems are made up of a series of connected business processes. This means that they essentially consist of multiple different business processes that need to be worked through in order to perform a particular business function or achieve a specific outcome for your business.

In a bookkeeping context, you will usually have clearly defined systems in place around different aspects of your business, such as how you plan, manage your people, develop and implement processes, and utilise technology. Some examples of business systems could be client relationship management (CRM) systems, people management systems, or practice management systems. Each one of these will consist of multiple different business processes that make up this broader system.

## Why are they important?

Having the right systems and processes in place is important for many reasons. For example:

- They help to create consistency within the business: By having well-defined systems and processes in place, you can ensure that tasks are carried out consistently every time by different team members and different teams.

- They help to create clarity: Having the proper systems and processes in place can help to create clarity around how different tasks should be carried out and why. This can also create clarity around people's roles and responsibilities within the business – for example, what each person is responsible for, who reports to who, and what the hand-off points are for different tasks.

- They help to streamline operations and identify opportunities for improvement: By having your processes and systems clearly mapped out and documented, it will be easier for you to identify areas for improvement. For example, what pain points or bottlenecks are currently creating inefficiencies within your business? Are there redundant, irrelevant, or unnecessary tasks or steps that are taking up your time, without actually adding any value to your business? Is there a better way to do things that would help you to do the same thing in an easier, faster, and more efficient way?

- They make it easier to onboard new staff: Any time that a new staff member comes on board, it is guaranteed there will be a learning curve as they adjust to their new role and responsibilities. However, having proper processes and systems in place can make this learning curve a little less steep. Rather than you having to spend time training new staff, they can simply refer to the systems and processes that have already been documented to get up to speed. Likewise, if one of your staff members have to go on leave, having these processes and systems can make it easier for someone to step into another's role temporarily without too much training required.

- They ensure legal and regulatory compliance: Many businesses are required to comply with certain legal and regulatory obligations, and bookkeeping practices are no exception. Having clear processes and systems helps to ensure that different tasks are being carried out in a way that is compliant with these legal and regulatory requirements.

- They can be scaled as the business grows: When you have the right processes and systems in place from the beginning, you will be able to easily adapt them to suit your business's changing needs as you grow.

In short, both systems and processes are essential for you to be able to drive growth efficiently and effectively for your bookkeeping practice. This is key if you plan to grow and scale your business, so having them in place from early on will make this process as smooth as possible for you.

**What systems and processes can you have?**

There are a number of different systems and processes that bookkeeping practices can have in place to ensure their smooth day-to-day operations, as well as to prepare them to scale and grow in the future. Although it wouldn't be possible to cover every possible system and process within the scope of this chapter, some of the systems and processes you are likely to need will include things like:

*Processes (for)*
- Setting goals and team targets
- Creating budgets
- Responding to customer enquiries
- Answering the phone
- Responding to emails – especially regular and recurring emails
- How certain financial reports should be prepared
- How accounts payable should be processed
- How payroll should be run
- Raising new invoices
- Writing blogs and articles
- Creating newsletters
- Posting to social media
- How different products or resources should be created (e.g. eBooks or templates)
- How you advertise job vacancies
- How you recruit staff
- How you onboard staff
- How you train staff
- Handling resignations or terminations
- Continuous improvement activities
- Managing complaints
- Customer onboarding and offboarding

- Managing customer files and privacy
- Performance management
- Flexible working arrangements.

*Systems (for)*
- Lead generation
- Proposals/quoting
- Practice management
- Payroll
- Creating and storing content
- Accounting and bookkeeping
- Document management
- Client relationship management (CRM)

Again, the specific types of processes and systems that you need in place for your bookkeeping practice will depend on a range of factors, such as your current size, future growth targets, number of staff, and the kinds of business activities you carry out. The above list should provide you with a good starting point. Remember, though, that they will evolve and change as new learnings happen!

**Creating your processes and systems**

Whenever you decide to create processes and systems for your bookkeeping practice, it is important that these are clearly defined and well outlined to ensure that the end product is easy to follow and can be used consistently by everybody in your business. There are a few key steps you should follow to help ensure this:

1. Set your goal: First of all, you will want to decide what your goal is for the process or system you are creating. For example, are you wanting to

streamline your current process to achieve the same result, but in less steps? Or are you wanting to reduce the amount of manual work and admin associated with your key business activities? Whatever your goal is, it is important to establish this early on as this will impact how your end process or system looks.

2. Identify key requirements: You will then want to identify the key requirements for your process or system. For example, are there key features, elements, or steps that it needs to include?

3. Planning: Once you have identified your goal and your requirements, it's time to start planning your process or system. This may involve mapping out a rough version of how you think the process or system should look, and sharing this with your team to get their feedback. This feedback step is an important one. Your team members will be the ones using the process or system, so it's important that they get to provide input into it. You might also gain insights into things like what they are looking for in the new process or system, as well as what they do and don't like about the current way of working. All of these things will influence your development of the new process or system.

4. Document it: Once you have gathered feedback from your team and planned how the process or system will look, you can then map it out in more detail. This means creating a detailed blueprint or roadmap for your process or system that shows:

o Each of the individual steps that make up the broader process

o The important details or elements for each step

o Who is responsible for each step of the process

o What tools or resources will need to be used at each step of the process

o Where the hand-off points are to different team members within the process

The key here is to make sure that your process or system is thoroughly documented, so that anyone who is not familiar with the process can pick it up and understand what it means – whether they are a new or existing staff member who is moving into a new role. Your blueprint or roadmap needs to clearly show all the above details, to ensure that all of your team members know exactly what needs to be done at each step of the process.

5. Implementation: Once your process or system has been mapped out, it's time to implement it. This means communicating with your team about the new process or system that is being implemented, and setting the expectation that this will be followed from now on to create consistency in the way they carry out their day-to-day tasks. Of course, you should also lead by example and ensure that you are following the new process or system in the way you do your own work, as this will promote adoption and compliance across your team.

6. Review: Once you start implementing the process, you will almost certainly begin to notice opportunities to improve it. When you map your process out, you

might think that it will allow you and your team to work better and more efficiently. However, in practice, you might notice that it is not panning out as well as you hoped. For example, are there recurring issues or pain points that are emerging? Are there things about the process that you think you could change or improve to make it better? Are you achieving better productivity and saving time and money, or are people struggling and spending more time trying to catch up with the new process than they are adding value to your business? All of these things are important to notice and pay attention to.

7. Continue to seek feedback: As an extension of the previous step, it is important that you also continue to ask your team members for feedback about how they are finding the new system or process. Are they finding that it helps them to do their jobs better and more efficiently, or are they noticing bottlenecks and certain pain points that are getting in their way? What do they like and not like about it, and what would they like to see changed or improved? All of these types of feedback will provide you with valuable insights that you can then use to refine and hone the process or system further until you arrive at the optimal state.

8. Modify the process: Once you have gathered feedback and made your own observations about the new process or system, you may find that you need to make refinements or changes to the way you mapped it out previously. Most often, processes and systems require a few iterations to get them absolutely perfect,

so don't be too hard on yourself if you find it takes a few tries to nail that new process or system. Simply take on board the feedback and observations you have received, identify opportunities for improvement, make the necessary changes, and have another go.

Once you have developed your processes and systems, the last thing to do is to store them. It is no use storing your systems and processes in your head, or in some other obscure location that nobody knows how to access. Storing your processes and systems in an easy-to-access central location will ensure that your staff know how to find them, and can refer back to them any time they are unsure about how a particular task should be done.

A key thing to remember: a failure is a broken process, nothing more, nothing less. I think this is important to remember when scaling and developing a team, as it is not an individual's failure, but merely a breakdown in process only. Never blame, just fix the process and implement; if breakdown occurs again, review the process and change it.

# Chapter 13: Making Strategic Investments

In addition to creating clearly defined processes and systems for your bookkeeping business, there are a few other things that you can do to streamline your operations and enhance your profitability. One of these is to make strategic investments in tools and resources that will make your job easier and allow you to achieve a greater level of efficiency and productivity.

### Investing in software

One example of a strategic investment you could make would be investing in specific software that allows you to carry out your day-to-day business activities with more ease. Most bookkeeping practices will already use some kind of financial management software such as Xero, MYOB, or QuickBooks. Some other strategic investments you might make could be some of the following:

- Client relationship management system (CRM)
- Document management system (DMS)
- Practice management software
- Communication tools
- Time tracking and billing software
- Payment processing system
- Data backup and security
- Proposal software
- Reporting and analytics tools
- Marketing and social media management
- Client portal

One of the strategic investments I made was using a practice management software which tracks staff time and efficiency. Staff time is how you multiply your income, and seeing what percentage of time is spent on client tasks versus admin tasks is vital because if you can tweak the efficiency ratio, your gross profit changes significantly.

Another situation, which in hindsight was a massive lesson, is that we started with a specific document and email management system because I wanted to be modern and thought it was a good solution. However, we ended up changing to an older, more trusted provider as it integrated with more services. Since then, we have not looked back as our whole practice utilises all the add-ons for that provider instead of needing different software programs for this and that.

**Investing in automation**

Another example of a strategic investment could be automation. This is definitely something that I'd recommend looking into, because there are tons of ways that you can automate processes for bookkeeping practices.

In fact, one report from McKinsey estimates that around 60% of occupations can automate at least 30% of their activities – and I would certainly say that bookkeeping is one of those occupations! Many software programs and platforms now include automation functions, meaning that a lot of time-consuming, repetitive tasks (such as data entry) that previously had to be completed manually can now be performed automatically in seconds, at the simple touch of a button.

Although software and automations cost money, I would definitely say they're an investment that is worth making for your business. The right automations will help you to streamline your operations, become more efficient, and save time, leaving you time to take on more high-value tasks that will generate profit for your business.

**Investing in experts**

Sometimes, it will be necessary to call in the help of an expert. Although as business owners, it can be tempting for us to try and do everything ourselves, it is often in the best interests of our business to pay for an expert – particularly when we are unsure how to do something or have not done it before. In my opinion, this is definitely something worth investing in.

There might be times when you want to offer a particular service but don't know how to deliver it, in which case you might find it helpful to work with a mentor or specialist to learn how to offer this to your clients. As a couple of examples, I hired a sales expert to train me and show me how to create sales scripts and make calls, what to listen out for, and how to move a client through the sales funnel. This training was invaluable and I have looked at sales in a whole new way since.

I also engaged a marketing expert to help me with this side of the business. Remember how early on in my business journey, I spent a large amount of money on wasted marketing activities? This happened because I didn't understand the client–marketing relationship. By engaging someone to complete customer profile mapping, I began to identify the wants, desires, and pain points for my ideal clients. On the back of the customer profile mapping, I now use a marketing strategist to help align my business's marketing elements so that they work together. This has flowed through my entire marketing strategy now, and has significantly increased our enquiries and client numbers.

Another example of a time when it might be worth calling in an expert is when developing your processes and systems. Because these play such an important role in providing your business with a solid foundation for future growth and scaling, they are definitely something that you shouldn't scrimp on in my opinion. If your budget allows for it, I would absolutely advise paying for an expert to help you with your systems and processes early on.

In my personal experience, I have found that when you try and develop processes and systems yourself from scratch, you often end up with something half-baked that you then have to go back and redo later on, particularly when you haven't had experience in creating processes and systems before. Or perhaps what you thought was the best way ends up not being so after all, and you realise after investing a lot of time and money in a particular system that there is another quicker, easier way to do things. You might not realise this until you reach the next revenue hurdle, but you will still eventually find this out the hard way and have to go back and do everything again.

Whatever the issue, working with an expert who has experience in developing processes and systems for businesses of all sizes, especially bookkeeping businesses, is a great way for you to overcome these issues. Someone who has developed effective and efficient processes and systems for bookkeeping practices in the past will be able to advise you on the best ways to carry out different tasks within your business and will also be able to recommend different software, automations, and systems to make day-to-day life at your business run more smoothly. This way, you will save yourself many headaches, as well as a lot of time and money in the long run for both you and your business by not having to do things twice.

# Chapter 14: Scaling Up - From Generalist to Niche Success

Once you hit the $250–500k mark, you will be well into the process of scaling up your business. At the same time though, you will also be at the point when you can afford to start refining your service offerings, and honing in more specifically on a particular niche.

## Bookkeeping specialisations

When you first start your bookkeeping business, it is likely that you will need to offer a broader, more general range of services. When starting out, you will usually find that you need to do this in order to attract as many new clients as possible, and generate enough business and money to keep your business afloat.

Over time though, as your business and profits grow, there will be more scope for you to move away from general practice and specialise in a particular area. Although this may not be the right choice for every bookkeeper (as some prefer to remain as general practitioners), for many, part of achieving their "why" means becoming an expert or specialist in their areas of interest. Becoming a specialist in a certain area of bookkeeping means that you will no longer have to offer services that you do not enjoy or which do not add value for you and your business. Instead, you can focus on offering only those services that align with your interests, and which create value and help you to take your business to where you want it to be.

There are many different areas that you may choose to specialise in at your bookkeeping business. Some of the common ones include:

- Business bookkeeping: Business bookkeeping practices specialise in working with businesses and companies of all sizes. They offer their bookkeeping services exclusively to businesses, not individuals, and will usually offer comprehensive solutions that allow businesses to outsource their finance function so they do not need to carry this out in house. Within the realm of business bookkeeping, you could hone this down even further – for example, do you want to specialise in working with sole traders, companies, small businesses, or larger organisations? You could also focus on businesses of certain sizes, or those which generate a certain amount of revenue and turnover.

- Occupation- or industry-specific bookkeeping: You may also decide to specialise in offering bookkeeping services for a particular type of industry or occupation. An example of this could be medical bookkeeping, which is a specialisation that is relatively common in the bookkeeping field. Medical bookkeepers work exclusively with medical centres, doctors, and other medical practitioners to take care of all their bookkeeping needs. As an extension of this, you could also work exclusively with clients in another industry or occupation that interests you – for example, bookkeeping services for female entrepreneurs or for tradies.

- Accounts payable and receivable services: Likewise, you could specialise in providing accounts payable and accounts receivable services for businesses. This could mean processing their invoices, paying their bills, reconciling transactions, and following up on unpaid bills and debts.

- Not-for-profit bookkeeping: Not-for-profit organisations have their own specific regulatory and reporting requirements that they need to comply with, which can be quite different to for-profit organisations. With this in mind, if you have experience in delivering bookkeeping services to not-for-profit organisations, you could position yourself as a specialist in bookkeeping for this type of organisation.

- Age-specific bookkeeping: You could also offer specific bookkeeping services for a certain age group, or education services designed for improving financial literacy in these age groups. For example, you could specialise in working with young people who are just entering the workforce or starting their own businesses, or older people who are running their own family businesses but who need some help with their books.

- Payroll services: Some bookkeepers may position themselves as specialists in payroll, and only offer this service rather than other more general bookkeeping services. This may be a drawcard to some businesses who do some of their bookkeeping in house, but who wish to outsource their payroll function.

- Financial reporting: This is another thing you could choose to specialise in as a business. All businesses will need to prepare some kind of financial reporting, though the legal and regulatory compliance requirements in place around this will vary from business to business. Balance sheets, cash flow statements, and profit and loss statements are just a few of the things you could be helping your clients with as a specialist in financial reporting.

- Software set-up services: Some businesses may not want to carry out their bookkeeping in house and may prefer to outsource this function entirely. However, they might need some help setting up their accounting systems and software programs, or need some training on how to use these platforms. If you are a whiz in Xero, QuickBooks, MYOB, or other accounting software, you could specialise in getting businesses set up and trained in how to use these systems in house.

- Coaching, consulting, and training: Rather than offering bookkeeping services yourself, you could also take more of a hands-off role by positioning yourself as a coach, trainer, or consultant. For example, if you are very experienced in the field, you could train or coach other bookkeepers – either on the technical aspects of bookkeeping or the logistics of how to run your own successful bookkeeping practice. You could also take on more of a consulting role, and advise other bookkeeping practices on how to achieve financial success and maximise the smooth day-to-day running of their operations.

- Products rather than services: This ties into what we were talking about in the earlier chapters of this book, where we spoke about deciding whether to operate as a bookkeeping practice or as a bookkeeping company.

You will recall that operating as a company means that rather than providing bookkeeping services to your clients personally, you might be selling products and services they can use themselves. For example, you could sell eBooks, online courses, templates, printables, and other online resources to help your clients master some aspect of bookkeeping for themselves. Selling products can be a great way to diversify your income and create an additional revenue stream.

- Advisory services: Bookkeeping practices offering advisory services position themselves as trusted advisors for anything to do with their clients' business and finances. Many will employ accountants and other business and finance specialists so that they can take on a higher-value role that exceeds the scope of a traditional bookkeeping practice. They are then able to offer a more comprehensive range of services to add real value for clients and their businesses – for example, business and financial goal setting, setting key performance indicators (KPIs), financial health evaluations, year-end financial statement preparation, regulatory compliance, strategic planning, assessing profitability, cash flow forecasting, budgeting, industry benchmarking, strategy, financial analysis, financial decision making, and risk management. This positions the bookkeeping practice as an end-to-end solution for their clients' business and finance needs, as well as an authoritative source of answers to any questions their clients have about their business and finances.

As you can see, there are many different pathways that your bookkeeping business can take when it comes to the area in which you wish to specialise. I would recommend starting with defining who your ideal client is, and then working your way up to finding your specialisation from there. Ask yourself, what specialist services would be of the most value to your ideal client, or what kind of expert advice would they be looking for in relation to their businesses? This will help you to identify some potential areas in which you may like to specialise.

By thinking carefully about your ideal client and your "why", and evaluating your vision, goals, priorities, and values as a business, you will be able to identify the pathway that is most attractive to you.

## Why specialise? The challenges and benefits

When deciding whether you want to specialise in a particular area of bookkeeping or not, there are a number of challenges and benefits that you will need to take into account. There are advantages and disadvantages of both specialising and practising as more of a general business which are important for you to recognise and understand before you can make a fully informed decision about where you want to take your business.

In terms of the benefits of specialising in a particular area, these include that you can make a name or brand for yourself as being a specialist or expert in a particular area of bookkeeping. You will also likely be able to command higher fees for your services, given you possess unique specialist expertise beyond that of many other bookkeepers. You will also usually be able to offer more tailored solutions that align closely with the needs, wants, and requirements of your clients, rather than offering one-size-fits-all solutions that are designed to meet the needs of "everybody".

However, the drawback of operating as a specialist is that you may have access to a narrower base of potential clients, as you will be appealing only to clients who are looking for the particular service or expertise that you offer, rather than those who are looking for bookkeeping services more generally. Remember though that your goal here is not necessarily to appeal to everyone – it is to connect with ideal clients who can create the most value for you and your business, and to whom you can offer the most value in return.

On the other hand, you also have the option to operate as a general practitioner or generalist. Some of the benefits of taking this approach to running your bookkeeping practice include that you will be able to appeal to a broader range of potential customers, given you'll be offering a variety of different bookkeeping services designed to meet the needs of all kinds of customers. This means that you may find it less challenging to find new business than someone who only offers a few more specialist services.

However, the drawbacks of this kind of approach include that your professional abilities will be less unique than bookkeepers who are experts or specialist in a particular area. This means that there will be many other bookkeepers out there who offer the same services as you do, which may make it harder for you to stand out from the competition. Also, you may find it harder to focus on your ideal clients, as you will be servicing such a broad range of client types across all of the different services that you offer that it may be difficult to hone in on just one.

As you can see, there are definitely advantages and disadvantages to both approaches. Personally, my advice would be to look for opportunities to specialise or make your business stand out in some other way from your competitors, as this will increase your capability to maximise your profits and achieve your "why". Also, if your goal is to grow and scale, your ability to do this will be limited if you offer too many services and are not specific enough about what you offer. It will be far easier for you to scale if you specialise in perhaps three or four services that you do really well, compared to if you offer a huge menu of twenty or thirty services. For this reason, I would strongly advise becoming a specialist over operating as a generalist if scaling your bookkeeping business is your goal after you have passed the survival threshold where you take on all clients in order to survive.

With that said, the decision as to whether to specialise or generalise is a personal one that you need to make, factoring in your business goals and what is in the best interests of your business. For many bookkeepers, the goal may be to scale up, while for others, though, growth may be less of a priority.

### Exercise: Identifying what you do and don't do

This is something that I messed up big time. When I first started out, I was very general and my services were all over the shop, which meant that I was also all over the place in my branding and marketing. Essentially, I was advertising "everything" to "everybody", which meant I ended up offering a lot of services to clients who didn't add any real value for me and my business. It was only later when I took a long, hard look at where my business was at and where I wanted to get to that I realised I needed to be more selective and really niche down to get to where I wanted to be.

It's usually when you get to around the $250–500k mark that you will be able to start being more selective and really refine what you do. This will ensure you are only working with the ideal clients with whom you want to work and are only offering the services you want to offer, which add real value to your business.

For me, a key thing was identifying what we do and what we don't do. This was a very simple exercise where I took a piece of paper, drew a line down the middle, and really took a deep dive into what I did and didn't want to do as a practice.

On the "what we do" side, I had the services that:

- I enjoyed offering
- Were profitable
- Created value for me and my business
- Would allow me to scale
- I could automate or streamline through processes

On the "what we don't do" side, I had the services that:

- I found too stressful
- I didn't enjoy offering
- I didn't want to offer any more
- Would not easily scale
- Were time-consuming, and which I could not automate or streamline in any way

By completing this exercise, I found that I was able to get a very clear indication about what I did and didn't want to do as a business. For example, I knew that I wanted to work with larger businesses with a high level of turnover (what we do) rather than smaller businesses (what we don't do).

I also knew that my strengths were financial administration, reporting, accurate numbers, and ongoing compliance, so I knew these were areas where I could add good value for my clients. So, I identified these as some of my "what we do" services. However, I knew that I didn't enjoy working with clients who couldn't (wouldn't) pay, who would not take responsibility for their results and blame others, and who had no vision or desire to grow, so I put these clients on my "what we don't do" side.

I would strongly recommend that you do the same exercise to gain more clarity around what services you do and don't want to offer at your bookkeeping business. Just do what I did! Grab a piece of paper and draw a line down the middle, and write "What we do" at the top on one side and "What we don't do" at the top of the other side. Then, start running through your list of services and for each one, ask yourself: Is this something I want to continue offering or not?

Here are some other questions to ask yourself as you complete this exercise:

- What are all of the services that you currently offer to your clients?
- Of those, which services do you enjoy offering?
- Which services do you not like offering?
- Which services do you find stressful or dread doing?
- Which services are the most profitable for your business?
- Which services do you feel create the most value for you and your business?

- Which services are of the most value to your ideal clients?
- Which services will allow you to grow and scale?
- Which services can be automated or made easier in some way?
- Are there any services that you don't offer yet, but which you want to?
- Are there services that you can't offer yourself, but which you could bring someone else on board to offer?
- Are there client types or attributes you don't want to service?

By completing this exercise, you will quickly start to gain clarity around those services you do and don't want to be offering any more. For example, you might realise that you want to position yourself more as an advisory service and look after the finances of your clients' businesses with more of a big picture view. In this case, you'd put advisory on your "what we do" list, and put everything else on your "what we don't do" list.

Maybe you want to take on clients on more of an end-to-end basis so that each one of your jobs is higher value, and stop doing ad hoc, one-off, lower-value jobs for small clients. In this case, retainer work and bundles might go on your "what we do" list, along with larger clients who generate a certain amount of revenue. You might put smaller clients who do not generate that amount of revenue on your "what we don't do" list, along with ad hoc or one-off jobs.

Or you might realise that you've fallen out of love with traditional bookkeeping, and are looking for a new way to challenge yourself – for example, by offering consulting and training services or by stepping up into more of a business advisory role. This would mean that you would identify these as your "what we do" services, and put everything else (like payroll, accounts payable, accounts receivable, financial reporting, and so on) in the "what we don't do" bucket.

By the end of this exercise, you will have a clear roadmap for where you want to take your business moving forward, including which services you need to start or stop offering to get to where you want to be.

## How to stop offering certain services

This goes back to what we talked about previously, where we discussed how it is sometimes necessary to have difficult conversations with your clients. When you decide to stop offering certain services is one of those times, as you will obviously need to let your current clients know that you will no longer be offering the services for which you were previously engaged.

You will recall the previous example from the chapter on having difficult conversations:

*"It's been lovely working with you and your team. Unfortunately, I will no longer be able to offer x services to you, as I am no longer going to be offering this service. I apologise for the inconvenience, and would be happy to refer you on to another contact who will be better able to meet your needs."*

This is just one example of how you might choose to inform your clients that you have decided to stop offering certain services – by sending them a clear, professional email that notifies them that you have stopped offering that particular service. You could even add in another line or two there to talk about why you have decided to stop offering that particular service – for example: "*To ensure that I am able to continue to provide the very best standard of service to my bookkeeping clients, I have made the difficult decision to narrow down my service offering to focus on a few key services: x, y, and z. This means that I will no longer be offering any other bookkeeping services that fall outside this scope.*"

In your email to your clients, you should also clearly set out the date when you will stop offering these services. You might say something like: "*I will no longer be offering this service after x date*" or "*I will no longer be offering this service effective x date.*" Keep in mind that you should give your clients at least a month or two's notice so that they have time to engage another bookkeeper or work out an alternate solution now that you will no longer be working with them.

Finally, offering the client a referral to another bookkeeper or bookkeeping practice that does offer the service they want provides a nice "sweetener". Even though you are no longer able to help the client directly, you are still offering to help them to find another solution to their problems, which shows you still want to create value for them. This helps you to end your relationship with that client on the most positive note possible.

## Looking to the future

Once you've hit the $250–500k mark and have honed down your service offering, there is only one place left to look – and that is to the future.

You will recall that at the start of this book, we talked about some of the key milestones that you can expect to accomplish at different stages of your business. For example, when you get to $500k, it's going to be all about scaling. That means refining your pricing and your product to maximise your revenue, ensuring your processes are running as smoothly and efficiently as possible, and thinking about how you can target your ideal customers in the best possible way. When you get to $500–750k, you'll be thinking about how you can manage your relationships with key clients and referral partners. And finally, when you get to $750k+, you can start thinking about exiting the business and letting it run itself.

By doing these things, you can ensure you are doing all the groundwork to set your bookkeeping practice up for a successful and profitable future.

# In Conclusion

Thank you for taking the time to read this book. When writing this book, my goal was to take away some of the guesswork around what it takes to set up your own successful bookkeeping company, so I hope that it has achieved this for you.

I personally struggled at the beginning of my business journey, and learnt some significant lessons along the way that have helped me to get my business to where it is now.

My key takeaways from my business journey are that:

- Having a clear vision allows you to see where you are heading, so that you can then correct your journey's course any time things end up going a bit off track.
- Everything you choose to do and everything you don't is still a choice and sits solely with you. You can create whatever you choose.
- Referrals are key. Find people who have the same clients as you do, and find opportunities for you to collaborate in a mutually beneficial way.
- Invest in technology early and build for your vision – not where you are now.
- Invest in a team before you actually need one. Whether it's subcontractors or staff, doing this will allow you to maximise your returns, whilst allowing you to have more time to work on multiplier tasks.

- Breaking up with clients, suppliers, and team members is sometimes necessary, because you and your business are evolving and opening new opportunities. The ability to have difficult conversations is a muscle you need to exercise.
- Understand your ideal client and market yourself specifically towards them.
- Failure is nothing more than a learning experience, so reframe your way of thinking. If something doesn't go as expected, it's just a broken process that needs tweaking.

Wishing you all the best as you take the first steps towards making your dreams of starting a thriving bookkeeping business a reality!

If you would like more information, please feel free to:

- Reach out at renee@reneeminchin.com
- Join our Facebook group
- Subscribe to our live training offers
- Work with me by getting in contact

# Exercise: Planning How Your Bookkeeping Practice Will Look

To help you get started on your journey of starting your own successful bookkeeping business, I wanted to include this exercise to take you through what we have learnt about in each chapter step by step. By answering the following questions, you will start to get a clearer idea of how you want your bookkeeping business to look. You will then be able to put these ideas into action as you start taking the first steps towards starting your own bookkeeping business.

### Chapter 1: Create Your Vision

1. When you think about starting your own bookkeeping practice, what is it that you ultimately want to get out of it? This will help you to determine your "why".

2. What are your goals as a business? Think about what you would like to achieve as a business within the next three to ten years.

3. What are your values, or what are the things that you think are important?

4. What is your point of difference, or what makes you unique and stand out as a business?

5. Based on your answers to the previous three questions, what ideas do you have for possible vision statements for your business? Remember, you want something fairly concise – two or three sentences at most.

## Chapter 2: Defining What You Want and Where You Are Heading

1. Are you wanting to be more of a specialist or more of a generalist?

2. What services do you think you might want to offer?

3. Do you want to be hands on or hands off?

4. Will you be the only practitioner or will you hire other staff as well? If so, who?

5. Do you want to set up as a company or a practice?

6. What do you think are your biggest strengths, or what do you see yourself as being an expert or specialist in?

## Chapter 3: Identifying and Marketing to Your Ideal Client

1. What does your ideal client look like?

   a. What are their wants, needs, and preferences?

   b. What do they value?

   c. What age group are they in?

d. What area do they live in?

e. What gender are they?

f. What type of job do they do?

g. What kind of income do they earn?

h. What kinds of problems or struggles do they have?

i. What would make their lives easier?

j. What kinds of services do they want?

k. What is their budget for your services?

2. How do you think you could go about targeting your ideal clients in a strategic way? How will you be advertising or marketing yourself to them?

## Chapter 4: Launching Your Bookkeeping Business

1. What is your vision statement for your bookkeeping business? You might like to pick one from the ideas you were brainstorming earlier.

2. Who is your target market?

3. Who are your competitors?

4. What are your goals and objectives? What will some of your first major milestones be?

5. Will you be setting up as a sole trader, partnership, or company?

6. What will your business name be?

## Chapter 5: Pricing Strategies for Success | Chapter 6: Achieving Balance and Adjusting Pricing | Chapter 7: Overcoming the Fear of Raising Prices

1. Will you be charging by the hour or by the service?

2. What do you think your hourly rate will be (if you are charging by the hour)?

3. What do you think you might charge for different services (if you are charging by service)?

4. Will you be offering package or retainer rates? If so, what will this look like?

5. At what milestones do you think you will start to think about upping your prices?

6. What are some of the fears you currently have around raising your prices?

## Chapter 8: Do What You Love (and Delegate, Automate, or Eliminate the Rest!)

1. What are the different tasks that you will be doing on a day-to-day basis within your business?

2. Of these, which are some of the tasks you think you will delegate eventually?

3. Is there anything you think you could automate in your business?

## Chapter 9: Work Like a Snowball

1. What income hurdles are you going to be setting yourself?

2. What do you plan to achieve at each stage?

## Chapter 10: Building the Right Team | Chapter 11: Managing Difficult Conversations

1. What kinds of staff will you be hiring?

2. At what income hurdle will you start hiring staff?

3. Which team members will you hire first?

4. Will you be outsourcing or hiring in house?

5. What qualities will you be looking for in your team?

6. How will you go about hiring staff?

7. What kind of culture are you wanting to create for your staff? What kind of things will you value or what will you find important?

8. Will you be using a mentor or coach at all? What for?

## Chapter 12: Investing in Systems and Processes | Chapter 13: Making Strategic Investments

1. What processes do you have in place for your business?

2. What processes will you need to put in place for your business?

3. What about systems? Which ones will you have in place for your business?

4. Will you be using particular software?

5. Is there anything you think you will need to hire an expert to do?

## Chapter 14: Scaling Up – From Generalist to Niche Success

1. In which areas of bookkeeping do you want to specialise?

2. At what income hurdle will you start to become more specialist, rather than generalist?

3. Thinking back to the "Identifying what you do and don't do" exercise:

   a. What are some of the things you will do?

   b. What won't you do?

4. Which services will you eventually stop offering?